These End Times

Reconsidering Our Perceptions of What Lies Ahead!

Wayne Belcher

RIVER BIRCH PRESS

Daphne, Alabama

ISBN 978-1-951561-82-6 (print)
ISBN 978-1-951561-83-3 (e-book)

For Worldwide Distribution
Printed in the U.S.A.
River Birch Press
P.O. Box 868, Daphne, AL 36526

Table of Contents

Introduction

After finishing college and having found life to be somewhat boring as well as complex and often confusing, I decided to read my Bible to learn about God who created me. I soon discovered I had been ignorant of so much history of the creation and God's many works in the lives of all generations from Adam until today. My appetite to learn more about what God had already done suddenly became a driving desire to devour as much of His Word as I could. That was about fifty years ago, and I still have an inner hunger to discover what God is going to do or say today.

I have found myself to be somewhat like the Jews in Berea who received the Word of God. They "searched the scriptures daily, whether those things were so" (Acts 17:11). I search for proof of things I hear or read concerning God's Word. It just seems part of my spiritual makeup.

In these days which the Bible describes as perilous, it behooves us to search for certain truth in the multitude of information presented to the world daily. The Bible informs us of many dangers today through which we have to try to navigate our lives and beliefs correctly if we hope to be found faithful to God when judgment day arrives for us. This book is meant to help show you some major truths to encourage your quest to learn about our living God.

Because the Bible has informed us that the end times have already begun, this world, as we know it, has passed the half way point of its current type of existence. It is time to discover the depth of Father God's love for us in sending His only Son, Jesus Christ, to come to give His life sacrificially for our sins that we might have righteous standing before God. That is a great joy.

Because many have not fully read the Bible, this book is put forth to help guide us into truth. Explanations and warnings are needed to inform and protect us. By giving scriptural proof of some strong statements, this book is intended to edify readers to gain adequate information to be able to stand firmly on the truth.

A good translation of the Bible is better than a good paraphrase. A well respected minister recommended a translation of the New Testament by Charles B. Williams titled *The New Testament in the Language of the People.* Some students still enjoy the King James version of the Bible. Other sources can help when something seems too complex, but scripture can become a main daily drawing factor in life.

Not wanting to come short in the end is a driving force in the heart of this author to share spiritual truths discovered over the years. Your desire to grow in the truth is possibly what drew you to this book. God does not want any of us to perish. Therefore, be encouraged to take your time reading and considering what God has stated in His Word. He wants us to have an abundant life.

I

HEAD IN THE SAND

An alarming number of incidents have happened since the invention of the cell phone where people have paid dearly with their lives for failing to observe the dangers of their surroundings while using it.

People even risk their lives for something as simple as a selfie. For example, some people seem to be totally unaware of the possibility of being blown off the edge of a cliff by strong wind gusts when taking one. Others have been overconfident of their strength or uninformed of the conditions of a particularly dangerous place where they were climbing to take an interesting selfie.

Some have just been so rebellious that they have violated no trespassing signs about areas filled with danger. I have read of several people who have lost their lives due to lack of paying attention to warnings and their surroundings, all so they could take a selfie to amaze others. It seems like such a senseless loss.

In the spiritual realm, God wants us to know the condition of our relationship with Him. Is our relationship solid, or are we failing in ways many have before? Perhaps we have not realized that some actions are like quicksand.

Jesus Christ is the only way, absolute truth, and sacrificed life that Father God has provided for mankind to be forgiven and accepted by God. God has warned us about the presence of many deceptions and false prophets, apostles, christs, brethren, accusers, and doctrines. We should consider where our faith is placed because our whole life depends upon it.

Jesus warned about the danger of hearing about the things He spoke but not heeding them enough to become a doer of what is right.

Therefore whosoever heareth these sayings of mine, and doeth them, I will liken him unto a wise man, which built his house upon a rock: And the rain descended, and the floods came, and the winds blew, and beat upon that house; and it fell not: for it was founded upon a rock. And every one that heareth these sayings of mine, and doeth them not, shall be likened unto a foolish man, which built his house upon the sand: And the rain descended, and the floods came, and the winds blew, and beat upon that house; and it fell: and great was the fall of it (Matt. 7:24-27).

Since mankind has been given free will to choose what to believe, our eternal future is our own responsibility. Jesus Christ is the only true Messiah. He is not just a prophet. He is the solid rock, the true cornerstone on which to place our faith. Several scriptures highlight the great significance of His being the only cornerstone of a foundation for our faith and hope of salvation.

Therefore thus saith the Lord GOD, Behold, I lay in Zion for a foundation a stone, a tried stone, a precious corner stone, a sure foundation: he that believeth shall not make haste. Judgment also will I lay to the line, and righteousness to the plummet: and the hail shall sweep away the refuge of lies, and the waters shall overflow the hiding place (Isa. 28:16-17).

Jesus saith unto them, Did ye never read in the scriptures, The stone which the builders rejected, the same is become the head of the corner: this is the Lord's doing, and it is marvellous in our eyes? (Matt. 21:42)

And are built upon the foundation of the apostles and prophets, Jesus Christ himself being the chief corner stone; In whom all the building fitly framed together groweth unto an holy temple in the Lord: In whom ye also are builded together for an habitation of God through the Spirit (Eph. 2:20-22).

Wherefore also it is contained in the scripture, Behold, I lay in Sion a chief corner stone, elect, precious: and he that believeth on him shall not be confounded. Unto you therefore which believe he is precious: but unto them which be disobedient, the stone which the builders disallowed, the same is made the head of the corner, And a stone of stumbling, and a rock of offence, even to them which stumble at the word, being disobedient: whereunto also they were appointed (1 Pet. 2:6-8).

It is important to examine where we may have wrongly placed our faith. If we have built our spiritual house, our spirit man, upon the sand of false doctrine, then we can be certain to expect only destruction. Sand is abundant in this world. Some of us have chosen to believe the lies of false doctrines, religions, prophets, and saviors.

Some of us have even placed our hope in a particular church, denomination, or even in a close family member's religious reputation rather than in the Lord Jesus Christ. We may have our heads so far into the sand that we refuse to pull them out to even consider the possibility that we have made a mistake and are headed for hell.

Some sand is quicksand that sucks us deeper and deeper down so that we cannot get out without help. If we have not repented of our sins and put our faith in Jesus Christ as our Savior, then we are encouraged to do it now. God still wants everyone to be saved, but many never will be.

How could we be missing God's best and His blessings? Seducing spirits and false ministers are quite proficient in deceiving people. We may be putting our faith in a particular person who uses smooth words to draw people after himself or herself rather than leading them to Jesus Christ.

"The words of his mouth were smoother than butter, but war was in his heart: his words were softer than oil, yet were they drawn swords" (Ps. 55:21). Such deception may lead us to be so loyal as to be quite defensive of the one we have put our trust in, possibly even becoming angry and filled with hate against outsiders.

Some of us are indoctrinated from a very early age to follow a false religion and thus remain faithful to it throughout adulthood. "Train up a child in the way he should go: and when he is old, he will not depart from it" (Prov. 22:6).

Some of us may have been lied to by one or more false prophets. False prophets are often interested in acquiring other people's money and being held in high esteem by others. False prophets give false hope. They probably believe their own lies and blame others when their prophecies fail to come to fulfillment.

Jesus used a parable to warn about some of the dangers that hinder people from trusting in Him for salvation.

A sower went out to sow his seed: and as he sowed, some fell by the way side; and it was trodden down, and the fowls of the air devoured it. And some fell upon a rock; and as soon as it was sprung up, it withered away, because it lacked moisture. And some fell among thorns; and the thorns sprang up with it, and choked it. And other fell on good ground, and sprang up, and bare fruit an hundredfold. And when he had said these things, he cried, He that hath ears to hear, let him hear (Luke 8:5-8).

The disciples did not understand what Jesus was trying to tell them, so they asked the meaning of His parable. He explained that the devil takes the word of truth out of the hearts of some people who have heard it.

Others believe the truth for a while but fall away from the truth during times of temptation. The third group that fell among thorns are those people who have heard the truth but are so engrossed in the cares of life, riches, and pleasures in this world that they become spiritually unfruitful. And the final group is the only group that kept the Word in their hearts and became spiritually fruitful.

It is time to examine our own hearts and faith. Is our faith in our pastor or another minister, perhaps an apostle or a prophet? Is our religion considered a false religion by those of Christian faith who honor Jesus Christ by doing good works and speaking the truth?

Are we wrapped up in our cares for our own lives, trying to get rich and satisfy ourselves with pleasures? Have we fallen into evil due to temptations in life?

Have we lost all concept that Jesus Christ created all things that are created, and we have been sinners who need salvation? Ask God for His wisdom, knowledge, and understanding and then read Romans 1:18-32 slowly enough to gain understanding of this truth from God.

That scripture informs us that God has manifested the knowledge of Himself to all mankind. He also states that the invisible things have not been hidden but can be understood by the things He has made. Therefore, man has no excuse when choosing not to believe in Him.

Some have chosen not to believe in Him as God. They have rather chosen to believe that God is a similar being to ordinary man, capable of also being corrupted like man, or a being similar to some animal. Such people have been left to their uncleanness. They rejected the truth of God. Some also reject the sanctity of marriage and embrace homosexuality. Such have been saddled with a reprobate mind.

And even as they did not like to retain God in their knowledge, God gave them over to a reprobate mind, to do those things which are not convenient; Being filled with all unrighteousness, fornication, wickedness, covetousness, maliciousness; full of envy, murder, debate, deceit, malignity; whisperers, Backbiters, haters of God, despiteful, proud, boasters, inventors of evil things, disobedient to parents, Without understanding, covenantbreakers, without natural affection, implacable, unmerciful: Who knowing the judgment of God, that they which commit such things are worthy of death, not only do the same, but have pleasure in them that do them (Rom. 1:28-32).

If we still do not understand that scripture, then we need to repent of our sins and ask Jesus Christ to enter our hearts to save us, for the punishment of our sin is death. We need to spend time getting to know Jesus Christ personally.

We should turn away from our old lifestyle, our ungodly friends, our lusts, and the familiar places where we often produced evil in our lives. We will either love God or love money. We have to decide, because we will hate the other. Choose to love God.

We need to find some Christians that have lived their lives doing good things. Ask their advice about a good church to attend. Study the Bible, the Word of God. A good way to start is to read the New Testament.

If we have heard that some Christians refer to the group that we have been associated with as being a cult or false religion, we need to spend some time with our head out of the sand so that we can get God's viewpoint and opinion about that group. The living God who created us wants us to get to know Him and to have a good life.

There are only two places to go after a person dies. One is heaven, and the other is hell. God's breath is what gave man life (Gen. 2:7). When a person dies, the spirit of man still exists and is conscious, but they are not called being alive if it goes to hell.

It doesn't matter if we believe in hell or not. God has revealed in His Word that hell is the place for the unrighteous to go when they die, and hell is a place of torment.

Jesus told a story about a rich man and a beggar that sat at the rich man's gate. The rich man "fared sumptuously" according to Luke 16:19 while dogs licked the sores of the beggar whose name was Lazarus.

Lazarus died, and we are told angels transported him into what is referred to as Abraham's bosom (Luke 16:22). Afterward, the rich man died and arrived in hell. The rich man was in such torment that he begged Abraham to send Lazarus with some water to touch his tongue.

It seems appropriate here to insert a verse that describes the man's tongue. "And the tongue is a fire, a world of iniquity: so is the tongue among our members, that it defileth the whole body, and setteth on fire the course of nature; and it is set on fire of hell" (Jas. 3:6).

Abraham explained the two compartments for the dead at that time. The unrighteous were sent into hell where there is torment. The righteous, at that time, were in another compartment where there was water but no torment. None could pass from one compartment to the other.

The rich man wanted Abraham to send someone to warn his five brothers so they could avoid eventually going to hell.

Abraham saith unto him, They have Moses and the prophets; let them hear them. And he said, Nay, father Abraham: but if one went unto them from the dead, they will repent. And he said unto him, If they hear not Moses and the prophets, neither will they be persuaded, though one rose from the dead (Luke 16:29-31).

The unrighteous do not just remain in hell. There is a second death called the lake of fire (Rev. 20:14). The unrighteous are cast into the lake of fire. It burns with brimstone, which is sulfur, and sulfur has a horrible odor when burned.

The second death is an eternal torment in fire, horrible odor, no comfort, no hope, no rest, no water, constant anguish, and eternal consciousness of loss and evil where the spirits of evil men are not considered living but just existing.

Heaven will be without sorrow, pain, loss, and grief. Where would we rather spend eternity?

We need to pay particular attention to our surroundings today, not only the physical but especially the spiritual. No one in hell with the rich man wants to be there, but their fate is decided.

Have we all solidified our faith in Jesus Christ by learning to be doers of the Word of God? In order to do that, we will have to know at least a little about what that entails.

II

OVERCOMING DEFEAT

There was a movie I barely remember about a long distance runner from a small country who competed in the Olympics. I think he was unfamiliar with most of what was going to be required of him in his competition. The strange thing was that the movie was based on a true story, if I remember correctly.

The critical point near the end happened when this man, who was now the leader of the race, reentered the arena grounds for the last lap. When he did, the multitude of people began applauding him. He stopped running and started looking at those applauding him. He did not realize that he had not crossed the finish line. Other runners soon passed him. I think his naiveté set him up for the great disappointment of losing the race he had been leading just before the finish line.

Sometimes life can seem like a long succession of defeats. God has given us His Word, the Bible, filled with examples to help us learn how we should be able to live victoriously. Many ministers do not preach the whole Bible to their congregations, so the only solution is for people to read the Bible for themselves. Just examining a few scriptures can enlighten us to some of the important things to do and the things to avoid.

We are told that Eve was deceived by the devil, but Adam willfully disobeyed God (Gen. 3:6, 13). God spoke specific things to each of them (Gen. 3:16-19). They were subsequently driven from the garden of Eden and thus away from the tree of life (Gen. 3:23-24). However, it was for their good that He kept them from partaking of the tree of life. If He had allowed them to eat of it, they would have lived forever as sinners (Gen. 3:22).

That shows that God loved those creatures made in His image. He did not want them stuck with sin for eternity. God saw fit to enlighten us more in the book of Hebrews.

> *For whom the Lord loveth he chasteneth, and scourgeth every son whom he receiveth. If ye endure chastening, God dealeth with you as with sons; for what son is he whom the father chasteneth not? But if ye be without chastisement, whereof all are partakers, then are ye bastards, and not sons* (Heb. 12:6-8).

God, who is love, responded in loving compassion in order to help all of mankind, since Adam and Eve were our original ancestors (Gen. 3:20; Acts 17:26). However, Jesus' Father was and is God. God desired that every person would seek Him and find Him (Acts 17:27). Sin was the cause of Adam and Eve's defeat, but God provided the sacrifice of Jesus Christ as the only solution for mankind's sin problem.

When Joshua led Israel to war against Jericho, he warned them not to take accursed things for themselves. One man, Achan, of the tribe of Judah, did take forbidden things. Afterwards, when Joshua sent men to attack the city of Ai, Israel was greatly defeated. God revealed the identity of the man, and Achan confessed his sin.

Achan and his family were stoned, killed, at God's command. Achan's sin had caused Israel to be defeated in battle and some men of Israel to die. Once again we see that sin was the cause of defeat. After the penalty for the sin was carried out against Achan and his family, Israel eventually defeated the people of Ai.

Is there a particular cause of war?

> *From whence come wars and fightings among you? come they not hence, even of your lusts that war in your members? Ye lust,*

and have not: ye kill, and desire to have, and cannot obtain: ye fight and war, yet ye have not, because ye ask not. Ye ask, and receive not, because ye ask amiss, that ye may consume it upon your lusts (Jas. 4:1-3).

There is the answer. War comes from lusts within mankind. That is sin.

Love not the world, neither the things that are in the world. If any man love the world, the love of the Father is not in him. For all that is in the world, the lust of the flesh, and the lust of the eyes, and the pride of life, is not of the Father, but is of the world (1 John 2:15-16).

God sent Israel to fight and take the land He had given them. Israel's wicked enemies were not about to give up the land where they lived, so Israel had to fight to obtain it.

There was an impotent man who had been unable to walk for thirty-eight years (John 5:5). Shortly after Jesus healed the man, He found him again and told him not to sin any more, or else something worse would possibly happen to him (John 5:14). Sin was the problem once again. Jesus was the source of victory over the previous defeat in the man's life.

In the Old Testament, God had provided plans for a temple to be built where all Israel would be able to give specific sacrifices to cover their sin. God chastened Israel in Haggai's days because they had taken great care of their own individual houses but let God's house lay waste (Hag. 1: 8-11).

God prophesied through Haggai to the people.

And I called for a drought upon the land, and upon the mountains, and upon the corn, and upon the new wine, and upon the oil, and upon that which the ground bringeth forth, and upon men, and upon cattle, and upon all the labour of the hands (Hag. 1:11).

They were defeated in their labors but didn't understand why until the word of the Lord was prophesied to them. Their sin in not caring for God's house was the reason for the drought over all the land. Obedience to God is shown once again to be of utmost importance.

Paul was once prevented by the Holy Spirit from going into Asia to preach and spread the gospel.

Now when they had gone throughout Phrygia and the region of Galatia, and were forbidden of the Holy Ghost to preach the word in Asia, After they were come to Mysia, they assayed to go into Bithynia: but the Spirit suffered them not (Acts 16:6-7).

Should we suppose that he may have felt defeated temporarily? He needn't have felt so because God had a better plan. God gave him a vision, which led him to go into Macedonia (Acts 16:9-10). Each life has purpose, and God gives input to the righteous. "A man's heart deviseth his way: but the Lord directeth his steps" (Prov. 16:9).

Even rain should be observed. Is the land getting too much rain, too little, or a good amount? We should pay attention. "He causeth it to come, whether for correction, or for his land, or for mercy" (Job 37:13). Christians, we should use our prayer time to address critical signs of our times in areas where we live. Christians have authority to speak to the weather, but we should do so using God's wisdom from above.

Idolatry is a very serious sin. Pay attention to what happened to Israel in scripture.

My people are destroyed for lack of knowledge: because thou hast rejected knowledge, I will also reject thee, that thou shalt be no priest to me: seeing thou hast forgotten the law of thy God, I will also forget thy children (Hos. 4:6).

God warned them and us.

Whoredom and wine and new wine take away the heart. My people ask counsel at their stocks, and their staff declareth unto them: for the spirit of whoredoms hath caused them to err, and they have gone a whoring from under their God. They sacrifice upon the tops of the mountains, and burn incense upon the hills, under oaks and poplars and elms, because the shadow thereof is good: therefore your daughters shall commit whoredom, and your spouses shall commit adultery (Hos. 4:11-13).

Spiritual adultery amounts to idolatry, and idolatry amounts to spiritual adultery. Israel reached a point where God proclaimed that they would not even find Him when they sought Him.

They will not frame their doings to turn unto their God: for the spirit of whoredoms is in the midst of them, and they have not known the Lord. And the pride of Israel doth testify to his face: therefore shall Israel and Ephraim fall in their iniquity; Judah also shall fall with them. They shall go with their flocks and with their herds to seek the Lord; but they shall not find him; he hath withdrawn himself from them (Hos. 5:4-6).

Sodom and Gomorrah are also examples God used to warn mankind.

Even as Sodom and Gomorrha, and the cities about them in like manner, giving themselves over to fornication, and going after strange flesh, are set forth for an example, suffering the vengeance of eternal fire (Jude 1:7).

Homosexuality and fornication were rampant there and unfortunately are acceptable to many today. Even a former president of the United States had the outside of the White House lit up with colored lights to show his support of homosexuality, but God is greater than man.

"Every way of a man is right in his own eyes: but the Lord

pondereth the hearts" (Prov. 21:2). "There is a way which seemeth right unto a man, but the end thereof are the ways of death" (Prov. 14:12). Check out Sodom's iniquity:

> *Behold, this was the iniquity of thy sister Sodom, pride, fulness of bread, and abundance of idleness was in her and in her daughters, neither did she strengthen the hand of the poor and needy. And they were haughty, and committed abomination before me: therefore I took them away as I saw good* (Ezek. 16:49-50).

Shouldn't we look carefully to see if we have fallen in any of those areas? If we have, we should confess our iniquity, sins, and transgressions to Jesus Christ. "If we confess our sins, he is faithful and just to forgive us our sins, and to cleanse us from all unrighteousness" (1 John 1:9).

Read the following scripture to see how other lands had become polluted by man's sin.

> *Son of man, when the house of Israel dwelt in their own land, they defiled it by their own way and by their doings: their way was before me as the uncleanness of a removed woman. Wherefore I poured my fury upon them for the blood that they had shed upon the land, and for their idols wherewith they had polluted it: And I scattered them among the heathen, and they were dispersed through the countries: according to their way and according to their doings I judged them* (Ezek. 36:17-19).

We can also read in Ezekiel 16 how Jerusalem became polluted spiritually. Cities, nations, and individuals can be deceived and turn away from the living God, much to their unending regret if they remain so. Today the devil is working harder than ever in an attempt to defeat God and His holy people.

Repentance, confession of sin, prayer, and watchfulness are called for today to guard our lives and those of our families, friends, and neighbors. Many believers have lived before us and are now enjoying living eternally in God's presence. They suffered through life too.

We should maintain our faith, even when our pathways seem blocked, supplies haven't arrived, we are surrounded by evil adversaries, and we haven't seen a breakthrough yet. Acquire the attitude of Habakkuk:

Although the fig tree shall not blossom, neither shall fruit be in the vines; the labour of the olive shall fail, and the fields shall yield no meat; the flock shall be cut off from the fold, and there shall be no herd in the stalls: Yet I will rejoice in the Lord, I will joy in the God of my salvation (Hab. 3:17-18).

God's promises are true.

But seek ye first the kingdom of God, and his righteousness; and all these things shall be added unto you. Take therefore no thought for the morrow: for the morrow shall take thought for the things of itself. Sufficient unto the day is the evil thereof (Matt. 6:33-34).

God promised rewards to those of the seven churches in Revelation who would overcome. He is no respecter of persons, so we can also expect rewards if we overcome and remain faithful unto Him.

We are not to let past defeats keep us from going forward spiritually. God commanded us to come boldly before His throne. God also has told us that though the righteous man falls seven times, he will get back up again (Prov. 24:16).

If there seems to be some setback or hindrance, perhaps it is time to seek God in prayer to learn in what direction He wants us to go or how to proceed. Sometimes fasting or repentance is required to gain spiritual understanding of God's view of a situation.

We are not to let anything keep us from going to our heavenly Father's house for love, comfort, or wisdom. His words to us are spirit and life.

III

ABIDING IN GOD'S LOVE

When I fished in a little pond one time, the thought came to me to command the big fish to take my hook. My family was with me, so I was glad to have witnesses. Fairly quickly after I pronounced my command, a fish took my baited hook and raced back and forth across the pond with it.

I could hardly wait to land my big fish. As I reeled the line in, the fish got closer and closer to me, but I still had not even seen it. Excitement increased! When the fish was almost next to the little dock I was on, my line went slack.

I was so disappointed. After I reeled in the rest of the line, I discovered the power of the words I had spoken. The big fish had taken my hook right off my line!

Jesus marveled when he found a centurion with great faith, and the centurion's request was granted (Matt. 8:10). A woman who wanted Jesus to heal her daughter had great faith and was granted her request of Him (Matt. 15:28). Great faith is something that immensely pleases God.

After I realized that, I asked God to give me great faith in order to bring Him great joy or to please Him even more. From those two examples, we see that exercising great faith seems to surprise God, and it also results in appropriate answers to prayers associated with great faith.

"Even so faith, if it hath not works, is dead, being alone" (Jas. 2:17). Faith without good works is worthless. Faith's value

17

depends upon the good works that a person does. Therefore, we see that faith, even great faith if that is possible, cannot be of any value by itself since it is always dependent upon good works.

What about hope? "Hope deferred maketh the heart sick: but when the desire cometh, it is a tree of life" (Prov. 13:12). "A sound heart is the life of the flesh: but envy the rottenness of the bones" (Prov. 14:30). "A merry heart maketh a cheerful countenance: but by sorrow of the heart the spirit is broken" (Prov. 15:13).

"A merry heart doeth good like a medicine: but a broken spirit drieth the bones" (Prov. 17:22). A sick heart is a serious thing. "Trust in the Lord with all thine heart; and lean not unto thine own understanding" (Prov. 3:5). If our hearts are sick, we may fall short in trusting in the Lord with our whole heart.

We are warned about the importance of the heart. "Keep thy heart with all diligence; for out of it are the issues of life (Prov. 4:23). "Heaviness in the heart of man maketh it stoop: but a good word maketh it glad" (Prov. 12:25). The heart is so very important.

God has not left in dire straits His people whose hope has fallen short or has been deferred. He provides solutions for the heart and for hope. "The light of the eyes rejoiceth the heart: and a good report maketh the bones fat" (Prov. 15:30).

Spiritual light can be acquired by reading God's Word, and thus the heart can rejoice again. "Ointment and perfume rejoice the heart: so doth the sweetness of a man's friend by hearty counsel" (Prov. 27:9). Have you ever noticed how a man will become cheerful when he smells perfume on a lady? So also do a friend's proper words cheer a man.

"The Lord doth build up Jerusalem: he gathereth together the outcasts of Israel. He healeth the broken in heart, and bindeth up their wounds" (Ps. 147:2-3). Jesus Christ is an expert in knowing how to heal hearts that are broken.

But what about hope, the thing that was mentioned as being deferred and causing the heart to become sick? How do we get hope? "For whatsoever things were written aforetime were written for our learning, that we through patience and comfort of the scriptures might have hope" (Rom. 15:4). Thus those two ways—patience and scriptures—are methods to acquire hope.

We know we can read or listen to scriptures, memorize them, recall them, and recite them. Where then does one get patience? That is easy!

And not only so, but we glory in tribulations also: knowing that tribulation worketh patience; And patience, experience; and experience, hope: And hope maketh not ashamed; because the love of God is shed abroad in our hearts by the Holy Ghost which is given unto us (Rom. 5:3-5).

All you really need to gain hope is to suffer tribulation. Here we have seen that tribulation produces hope and that scripture can produce hope if you read or hear it. Which method do you prefer to gain your hope? Hope is dependent upon either tribulation or scripture.

Charity is the love translated from the Greek word *agape* (ag-ah'-pay). What is it dependent upon?

Charity, love, is so important that without it, speaking the tongues of men and angels; having the gift of prophecy; understanding all mysteries; having all knowledge; being able to remove mountains; giving all you have to feed the poor; and even giving your body to be burned are all fruitless to you (1 Cor. 13:1-3). Verses 4-8 of 1 Corinthians 13 reveals what this charity is like.

It:

suffers long
is kind
does not envy

does not exalt itself
is not puffed up
is not unseemly acting or rude
does not insist upon it's own rights
is not easily agitated
does not think evil thoughts
does not rejoice in iniquity
rejoices in truth
bears all things put upon it
believes all things possible by faith
hopes continually
endures all things
never fails.

Eight of those things refer to love's excellent qualities that it accomplishes or does. The other eight refer to the undesirable qualities that love does not participate in or experience.

What then is this amazing thing called charity or love? It appears to be an absolutely amazing commodity, the most amazing thing in existence. "He that loveth not knoweth not God; for God is love" (1 John 4:8). "And we have known and believed the love that God hath to us. God is love; and he that dwelleth in love dwelleth in God, and God in him" (1 John 4:16).

The word "love" in both of those verses is again that Greek word agape. This charity or love is speaking of the living God, and the truth He rejoices in is Jesus Christ. Is it any wonder that 1 Corinthians 13:13 states that charity is greater than faith and hope?

God is not dependent upon anything. He is the Truth we all should acknowledge and seek after while we are able. Jesus is the One who willingly came in human flesh in order to allow mankind to torture Him and hang Him on a tree so that He could become a curse for us. He did this to purchase our redemption from sin and death, for the penalty of sin is death.

Greater love hath no man than this, that a man lay down his life for his friends. Ye are my friends, if ye do whatsoever I command you (John 15:13-14).

How much have we been forgiven? Examine the following scripture to see if you can tell how much you have been forgiven, comparing yourself to how much you are able to love now.

Wherefore I say unto thee, Her sins, which are many, are forgiven; for she loved much: but to whom little is forgiven, the same loveth little (Luke 7:47).

Now think about how much we needed forgiveness before we became Christians. "For whosoever shall keep the whole law, and yet offend in one point, he is guilty of all" (Jas. 2:10). Did we ever keep the whole law before we were saved? Of course, we did not. Only Jesus Christ was ever able to keep the whole law. Therefore, we were guilty of breaking the whole law.

Are we able to determine how much we have been forgiven? Paul acknowledged himself as less than the least of all saints.

Unto me, who am less than the least of all saints, is this grace given, that I should preach among the Gentiles the unsearchable riches of Christ (Eph. 3:8).

Where do you think we belong in relation to other Christians? Are we greater than Paul who wrote much of the New Testament? Another very important verse should help us to be able to determine our current status. "If a man say, I love God and hateth his brother, he is a liar: for he that loveth not his brother whom he hath seen, how can he love God whom he hath not seen?" (1 John 4:20). The Greek word for love in that verse is *agapao*.

If we hate people, we don't love God. We don't have to like what people do or even like certain people, but we do have to love all people because they were created in the image of God.

We are warned to guard our hearts so that we do not become deceived and fall away from God. "And above all these things put on charity, which is the bond of perfectness" (Col. 3:14). Again, the word "charity" there is the Greek agape, so we are to put on Jesus Christ.

We are not to focus so much on life that we fail to remember God's love for us. It is all too easy to get excited about physical things and having fun. It can also be much too easy to get discouraged with life. God's promise of abundant life is especially filled with His love for us.

IV

GET UNDERSTANDING

When I used to work a swing shift, I would sometimes get a little groggy from lack of enough sleep. It really hit me hard one time in particular. I remember waking and suddenly becoming somewhat alarmed. I didn't want to be late for work.

I looked at the clock to see what time it was. I think it was sometime after six. Then I was totally confused. I quickly looked outside to determine if it was morning or night. Unfortunately, it was winter time when the sun sets early. I was at a total blank because of the darkness outside. I still did not know if it was morning or evening!

It is time for the church to grow into maturity. Do we dare put God at a lesser place than preeminence in our lives as this world is entering into a time like in the days of Lot? "Get wisdom, get understanding: forget it not; neither decline from the words of my mouth" (Prov. 4:5). God said that if we need His wisdom, then we have to ask for it (Jas. 1:5).

But if ye have bitter envying and strife in your hearts, glory not, and lie not against the truth. This wisdom descendeth not from above, but is earthly, sensual, devilish. For where envying and strife is, there is confusion and every evil work. But the wisdom that is from above is first pure, then peaceable, gentle, and easy to be intreated, full of mercy and good fruits, without partiality, and without hypocrisy (Jas. 3:14-17).

With that heavenly wisdom, we also need proper understanding. "Wisdom is the principal thing; therefore get wisdom: and with all thy getting get understanding" (Prov. 4:7). "How much better is it to get wisdom than gold! and to get understanding rather to be chosen than silver! The highway of the upright is to depart from evil: he that keepeth his way preserveth his soul" (Prov. 16:16-17). God will see ungodly peoples' souls and bodies destroyed in hell (Matt. 10:28).

Peter wrote that Paul had written some things that were hard to understand (2 Pet. 3:16). Although I have read hundreds of Christians books and articles, many by nationally recognized ministers, I cannot recall having ever read or heard about any of the extremely important, hard to understand things that Paul wrote.

James wrote that we have not because we do not ask God for what we want (Jas. 4:2). Ask God for understanding of His scriptures and His wisdom from above.

Look at some of Paul's writings in Romans:

Know ye not, that so many of us as were baptized into Jesus Christ were baptized into his death? Therefore we are buried with him by baptism into death: that like as Christ was raised up from the dead by the glory of the Father, even so we also should walk in newness of life (Rom. 6:3-4).

Have we been baptized? "Knowing this, that our old man is crucified with him, that the body of sin might be destroyed, that henceforth we should not serve sin. For he that is dead is freed from sin" (Rom. 6:6-7). "For ye are dead, and your life is hid with Christ in God" (Col. 3:3).

Our old man that we were before becoming saved is now dead. "Likewise reckon ye also yourselves to be dead indeed unto sin, but alive unto God through Jesus Christ our Lord" (Rom. 6:11).

"Now we know that what things soever the law saith, it

saith to them who are under the law: that every mouth may be stopped, and all the world may become guilty before God" (Rom. 3:19). Christians are no longer under the law of Moses because Jesus Christ fulfilled the law for us (Rom. 8:3-4). However, that does not mean that we should willfully choose to do wrong or evil. "What shall we say then? Shall we continue in sin, that grace may abound? God forbid. How shall we, that are dead to sin, live any longer therein? (Rom. 6:1-2).

Wherefore, my brethren, ye also are become dead to the law by the body of Christ; that ye should be married to another, even to him who is raised from the dead, that we should bring forth fruit unto God (Rom. 7:4).

Do we notice the part stating that Christians are dead to the law?

But now we are delivered from the law, that being dead wherein we were held; that we should serve in newness of spirit, and not in the oldness of the letter (Rom. 7:6).

Not only are we dead to the law, we are also delivered from it.

Paul wrote that sin slew him (Rom. 7:11). Then Paul began to explain a conundrum. He claimed to be carnal at that time (Rom. 7:14) even though he was one of the most spiritually mature believers. This is where we need to understand:

For that which I do I allow not: for what I would, that do I not; but what I hate, that do I (Rom. 7:15).

Now then it is no more I that do it, but sin that dwelleth in me (Rom. 7:17).

That is critically important to understand. Sin was doing things in Paul that Paul did not want to do. He followed up with an explanation:

For the good that I would I do not: but the evil which I would not, that I do. Now if I do that I would not, it is no more I that do it, but sin that dwelleth in me. I find then a law, that, when I would do good, evil is present with me (Rom. 7:19-21).

But I see another law in my members, warring against the law of my mind, and bringing me into captivity to the law of sin which is in my members (Rom. 7:23).

There were two laws contending with one another inside Paul.

"I thank God through Jesus Christ our Lord. So then with the mind I myself serve the law of God; but with the flesh the law of sin" (Rom. 7:25). The next verse (8:1) states that there is no condemnation for Christians who walk after the Spirit instead of walking after the flesh.

"For the law of the Spirit of life in Christ Jesus hath made me free from the law of sin and death" (Rom. 8:2). Even though he was experiencing the controversy within himself, he realized that it was not him sinning, but sin that dwelt within his flesh.

He even recognized that there was nothing good in his flesh (Rom. 7:18). The flesh of his body was carnal, but his mind was serving God! The condition of a person's mind is of critical importance. "For to be carnally minded is death; but to be spiritually minded is life and peace" (Rom. 8:6).

When Paul stated that he was carnal, he was recognizing the condition of his flesh, not the condition of his mind. With his mind, he was spiritual and walking after the Spirit.

Then he gave a clarification so that we could understand the conundrum found in each Christian's life.

But ye are not in the flesh, but in the Spirit, if so be that the Spirit of God dwell in you. Now if any man have not the Spirit of Christ, he is none of his. And if Christ be in you, the body is dead because of sin; but the Spirit is life because of righteousness (Rom. 8:9-10).

He stated the responsibility that Christians should mortify the evil deeds of the flesh, the body (Rom. 8:13).

Now, consider the writings of John.

Whosoever denieth the Son, the same hath not the Father: (but) he that acknowledgeth the Son hath the Father also. Let that therefore abide in you, which ye have heard from the beginning. If that which ye have heard from the beginning shall remain in you, ye also shall continue in the Son, and in the Father (1 John 2:23-24).

Pay attention to that little word "if." The word implies that people could choose to neglect to retain the way of salvation which they have heard from the beginning.

Because we have been given a free will, each person can choose what he or she wants to believe. Wrong belief is not necessarily sin, but specific wrong belief can cause some people to perish in hell and the lake of fire.

Now, let's see what John has to say about sin. "Whosoever committeth sin transgresseth also the law: for sin is the transgression of the law" (1 John 3:4).

Remember that Christians are no longer under the law. "Whosoever abideth in him sinneth not: whosoever sinneth hath not seen him, neither known him" (1 John 3:6). If we have maintained our faith in Jesus Christ and not grown lukewarm toward Him, then we are abiding in Him. Therefore, we are not sinning.

He that committeth sin is of the devil; for the devil sinneth from the beginning. For this purpose the Son of God was manifested, that he might destroy the works of the devil. Whosoever is born of God doth not commit sin; for his seed remaineth in him: and he cannot sin, because he is born of God (1 John 3:8-9).

There is that very significant point clarifying again that Christians do not sin. I do not see where quitting our belief is a sin, but it is utter foolishness, and sin certainly follows unbelief.

If and when a Christian turns away from faith in Jesus Christ, then that person will no longer be a Christian and can sin again and become like the dog that returns to his own vomit (2 Pet. 2:9-22). "We know that whosoever is born of God sinneth not; but he that is begotten of God keepeth himself, and that wicked one toucheth him not" (1 John 5:18).

One last scripture reference is in order to display here.

Blessed is the man that walketh not in the counsel of the ungodly, nor standeth in the way of sinners, nor sitteth in the seat of the scornful. But his delight is in the law of the Lord; and in his law doth he meditate day and night. And he shall be like a tree planted by the rivers of water, that bringeth forth his fruit in his season; his leaf also shall not wither; and whatsoever he doeth shall prosper (Ps. 1:1-3).

It did not state that only some of the things the blessed man does will prosper. Whatsoever things he does will prosper. Sinners will not prosper in all things because sin leads to death, so the scripture must be referring only to Christians.

Now we can understand the warfare that sometimes occurs within us. If we find sin in our flesh, we are to confess it to God. If we are serving God with our minds by believing in Jesus as our Savior, then we can have confidence we are still under His precious care.

V

DAY OF THE LORD

Sometimes we can misspell words. Do I want the word "flees" or "fleas?" What about the words "to," "too," or "two?" I heard of an incident where a couple thought they heard a particular word when a prophecy was given to them. Apparently, they took it to heart, believing God was sending them to Oregon. I never heard what they went through to get moved there.

The important thing was to understand what God wanted them to hear. I have no idea if they ever tested their prophecy or got pastoral counseling about it.

Later, I learned something important—sometimes what we have thought we heard may not have been true. It turned out that the prophecy to the couple actually included the word "organ," not "Oregon." They eventually returned to the city where they had heard the prophecy.

And we know that all things work together for good to them that love God, to them who are the called according to his purpose (Rom. 8:28).

That scripture is going to be extremely important until you leave this mortal world. I encourage you to memorize it to strengthen yourself for the days and nights ahead.

This long chapter contains many necessary truths. Please do not shortchange yourself by skipping lightly through them. This

29

information is vital for everyone's future. The many scriptures are presented so that the actual Word of God concerning the end times may be read. It is important to be aware of what is truth and what is falsehood about what you have heard and what you will hear in the future.

The scriptures will be numbered and separated for clarity and ease of reading. I have used bold fonts to highlight specific parts of many of the scriptures. My comments follow many of the verses and are in parentheses.

1. "**Prove all things**; hold fast that which is good" (1 Thess. 5:21). (It is each person's own responsibility to rightfully prove what is right and what is wrong.)

2. "Whoso keepeth the commandment shall feel no evil thing: and **a wise man's heart discerneth both time and judgment**" (Eccles. 8:5). (We can ask God for His wisdom.)

3. "These things I have spoken unto you, that in me ye might have peace. **In the world ye shall have tribulation**: but be of good cheer; I have overcome the world" (John 16:33). (Rom. 5:3 states that tribulation produces patience, and Heb. 10:36 states explicitly that we need patience.)

4. "**But of the times and the seasons, brethren, ye have no need that I write unto you.** For yourselves know perfectly that the day of the Lord so cometh as a thief in the night. For when they shall say, Peace and safety; then sudden destruction cometh upon them, as travail upon a woman with child; and they shall not escape. **But ye, brethren, are not in darkness, that that day should overtake you as a thief**" (1 Thess. 5:1-4).

5. "For **the time will come when** they will not endure sound doctrine; but after their own lusts shall they heap to themselves teachers, having itching ears; And they shall turn away their ears

from the truth, and shall be turned unto fables" (2 Tim.4:3-4). (I have heard of some strange things being taught in churches today.)

6. "Thou therefore **endure hardness, as a good soldier of Jesus Christ.** No man that warreth entangleth himself with the affairs of this life; that he may please him who hath chosen him to be a soldier" (2 Tim. 2:3-4). (It seems we all can relate to hardness in our lives.)

7. **"He that loveth his life shall lose it; and he that hateth his life in this world shall keep it unto life eternal"** (John 12:25).

8. "The Revelation of Jesus Christ, which God gave unto him, **to shew unto his servants things which must shortly come to pass;** and he sent and signified it by his angel unto his servant John:" (Rev. 1:1). (Revelation is a book revealing Jesus Christ, not the devil.)

9. "I am come in my Father's name, and ye receive me not: **if another shall come in his own name, him ye will receive"** (John 5:43). (That signifies that non-Christians will accept the antichrist.)

10. "So Christ was once offered to bear the sins of many; and **unto them that look for him shall he appear the second time** without sin unto salvation" (Heb. 9:28). (Jesus is to return a second time, but no third time is ever mentioned. Are you looking for Him?)

11. "And because iniquity shall abound, **the love of many shall wax cold. But he that shall endure unto the end, the same shall be saved"** (Matt. 24:12-13). (A person can go from being spiritually hot for Jesus Christ to lukewarm while in the process of growing cold.)

12. "So then because thou art **lukewarm,** and neither cold nor hot, **I will spue thee out of my mouth.** Because thou sayest, I am rich, and increased with goods, and have need of nothing; and **knowest not** that thou art wretched, and miserable, and poor, and blind, and naked" (Rev. 3:16-17).(A person must be in Christ and have Christ in himself in order to be saved.)

13. "And this gospel of the kingdom shall be preached in all the world for a witness unto all nations; **and then shall the end come.** When ye therefore shall **see the abomination of desolation, spoken of by Daniel the prophet, stand in the holy place,** (whoso readeth, let him understand)" (Matt. 24:14-15).

14. "So then faith cometh by hearing, and hearing by the Word of God. But I say, **Have they not heard?** Yes verily, **their sound went into all the earth, and their words unto the ends of the world"** (Rom. 10:17-18). (The gospel has already been preached in all the world.)

15. "Seventy weeks are determined upon thy people and upon thy holy city,

> **to finish the transgression,** and
>
> **to make an end of sins,** and
>
> **to make reconciliation for iniquity,** and
>
> **to bring in everlasting righteousness,** and
>
> **to seal up the vision and prophecy,** and
>
> **to anoint the most Holy"** (Dan. 9:24).

(I listed the verse that way to highlight the six things that will occur during the last week of the seventy weeks, where each week represents seven years.)

16. "So Israel rebelled against the house of David unto this day" (1 Kings 12:19). (The nation of Israel as a whole is still in rebellion against Jesus, a descendant of King David, though there are some Messianic Jews today.)

17. "O **Jerusalem,** Jerusalem, thou that killest the prophets, and stonest them which are sent unto thee, how often would I have gathered thy children together, even as a hen gathereth her chickens under her wings, and ye would not! Behold, **your house is left unto you desolate. For I say unto you, Ye shall not see me henceforth, till ye shall say, Blessed is he that cometh in the name of the Lord"** (Matt. 23:37-39).

18. "And he shall **confirm the covenant with many for one week: and in the midst of the week he shall cause the sacrifice and the oblation to cease,** and for the overspreading of abominations he shall make it desolate, even until the consummation, and that determined shall be poured upon the desolate" (Dan. 9:27).

(One week equals seven years there. The antichrist breaks his seven year covenant with Israel in the midst, possibly middle, of the seven years.)

19. "For then shall be **great tribulation, such as was not since the beginning of the world to this time, no, nor ever shall be.** And except those days should be shortened, there should no flesh be saved: but **for the elect's sake** those days shall be shortened. Then if any man shall say unto you, Lo, here is Christ, or there; believe it not. For **there shall arise false Christs, and false prophets, and shall shew great signs and wonders; insomuch that, if** *were* **possible, they shall deceive the very elect"** (Matt. 24:21-24).

(If all Christians were to be caught up already at the start of the seven years, then there would be no reason to shorten those days for the elect. Also, because much of the church has been taught that Jesus Christ is to return at the start of the seven year treaty with Israel, then those who believe that lie may very well believe the antichrist who comes on the scene is actually Jesus Christ.)

20. "For as the lightning cometh out of the east, and shineth even unto the west; so shall also the coming of the Son of man be" (Matt. 24:27).

21. "For as the lightning, that lighteneth out of the one part under heaven, shineth unto the other part under heaven; **so shall also the Son of man be** in his day" (Luke 17:24).

22. "And as it was in the days of Noe, so shall it be also in the days of the Son of man. They did eat, they drank, they married wives, they were given in marriage, until the day that Noe entered into the ark, and the flood came, and destroyed them all. Likewise also as it was in the days of Lot; they did eat, they drank, they bought, they sold, they planted, they builded; But the same day that Lot went out of Sodom it rained fire and brimstone from heaven, and destroyed them all. **Even thus shall it be in the day when the Son of man is revealed**" (Luke 17:26-30).

23. "**Immediately after the tribulation** of those days shall the **sun be darkened**, and the **moon shall not give her light,** and the **stars shall fall from heaven,** and the powers of the heavens shall be shaken: And **then shall appear the sign of the Son of man in heaven:** and then shall all the tribes of the earth mourn, and **they shall see the Son of man coming in the clouds of heaven with power and great glory. And he shall send his angels** with a **great sound of a trumpet, and they shall gather together his elect from the four winds, from one end of heaven to the other**" (Matt. 24:29-31).

(Notice this is after the tribulation period. From *Strong's*

Greek Dictionary 1588 "elect" also means "**chosen.**" This is when the dead in Christ and the living Christians are caught to meet Jesus Christ in the air. This scripture invalidates the pre-tribulation theory.)

24. "When the Son of man shall come in his glory, and all the holy angels with him, then shall he sit upon the throne of his glory: And before him shall be gathered all nations: and he shall separate them one from another, as a shepherd divideth his sheep from the goats: And he shall set the sheep on his right hand, but the goats on the left" (Matt. 25:31-33).

(Note that when Jesus returns, His angels are with Him, and He eventually sits upon His throne and divides the sheep nations from the goat nations.)

25. "Not as though the Word of God hath taken none effect. For **they** *are* **not all Israel,** which are of Israel: Neither, because they are the seed of Abraham, *are they* all children: but, In Isaac shall thy seed be called. That is, **They which are the children of the flesh, these** *are* **not the children of God:** but **the children of the promise are counted for the seed**" (Rom. 9:6-8).

(Faithful believers are the seed and thus the chosen, the elect.)

26. "For **he is not a Jew, which is one outwardly;** neither is that circumcision, which is outward in the flesh: But **he** *is* **a Jew, which is one inwardly; and circumcision** *is that* **of the heart, in the spirit,** *and* **not in the letter; whose praise** *is* **not of men, but of God**" (Rom. 2:28-29).

(That is why we can see that all Israel will be saved (Rom. 11:26). It is all the true Christians.)

27. "Howbeit that was not first which is spiritual, but that which is **natural;** and **afterward that which is spiritual**" (1 Cor. 15:46).

(Natural Israel came first. Spiritual Israel came afterward.)

28. "These shall make war with the Lamb, and the Lamb shall overcome them: for he is Lord of lords, and King of kings: and **they that are with him** *are* **called**, and **chosen**, and **faithful**" (Rev. 17:14).

(We have to remain faithful unto the end.)

29. "For this we say unto you by the word of the Lord, that we which are alive and remain unto the coming of the Lord shall not prevent them which are asleep. For **the Lord himself shall descend** from heaven with a **shout**, with the **voice of the archangel**, and with **the trump of God**: and **the dead in Christ shall rise first: Then we which are alive** *and* remain shall be **caught up together with them in the clouds, to meet the Lord in the air: and so shall we ever be with the Lord.** Wherefore comfort one another with these words" (1 Thess. 4:15-18).

(Being caught up is what some people refer to as the rapture.)

30. "And when he had spoken these things, while they beheld, **he was taken up; and a cloud received him out of their sight.** And while they looked stedfastly toward heaven as he went up, behold, two men stood by them in white apparel; Which also said, Ye men of Galilee, why stand ye gazing up into heaven? this same **Jesus, which is taken up from you into heaven, shall so come in like manner as ye have seen him go into heaven**" (Acts 1:9-11).

31. "And there shall be **signs in the sun, and in the moon, and in the stars;** and upon the earth **distress of nations, with perplexity; the sea and the waves roaring; Men's hearts failing them for fear, and for looking after those things which are coming on the earth:** for the powers of heaven shall be shaken. And **then shall they see the Son of man coming in a cloud with power and great glory**" (Luke 21:25-27).

32. "But of that day and hour knoweth no man, no, not the angels of heaven, but my Father only. But as the days of Noe *were*, so shall also the coming of the Son of man be. For as in the days that were before the flood they were eating and drinking, marrying and giving in marriage, until the day that Noe entered into the ark, And knew not until the flood came, and took them all away; so shall also the coming of the Son of man be" (Matt. 24:36-39).

(It will appear to be daily life as usual. Christians should rest in the Lord and be comforted by the Holy Spirit even when unbelievers do not seek or want Jesus Christ at His return.)

33. "And spared not the old world, but saved **Noah** the eighth *person*, **a preacher of righteousness**, bringing in the flood upon the world of the ungodly;" (2 Pet. 2:5).

(Only Noah's family was interested or desiring to be righteous when he preached.)

34. "**Who then is a faithful and wise servant**, whom his lord hath made ruler over his household, to give them meat in due season? Blessed *is* that servant, whom his lord when he cometh shall find so doing. Verily I say unto you, That he shall make him ruler over all his goods. **But and if that evil servant** shall say in his heart, My lord delayeth his coming; And shall begin to smite *his* fellowservants, and to eat and drink with the drunken; The lord of that servant shall come in a day when he looketh not for *him*, and in an hour that he is not aware of, And shall cut him asunder, and **appoint *him* his portion with the hypocrites: there shall be weeping and gnashing of teeth**" (Matt. 24:45-51).

(It is extremely important for us to be expecting and looking for Christ's return.)

35. "Then shall the kingdom of heaven be likened unto **ten**

virgins, which took their lamps, and went forth to meet the bridegroom. And **five of them were wise,** and **five** *were* **foolish.** They that were foolish took their lamps, and took no oil with them: But the wise took oil in their vessels with their lamps. While the bridegroom tarried, they all slumbered and slept. And at midnight there was a cry made, Behold, the bridegroom cometh; go ye out to meet him. Then all those virgins arose, and trimmed their lamps. And the foolish said unto the wise, Give us of your oil; for our lamps are gone out. But the wise answered, saying, *Not so*; lest there be not enough for us and you: but go ye rather to them that sell, and buy for yourselves. And while they went to buy, the bridegroom came; and they that were ready went in with him to the marriage: and the door was shut. Afterward came also the other virgins, saying, **Lord, Lord,** open to us. But he answered and said, Verily I say unto you, **I know you not. Watch** therefore, for **ye know neither the day nor the hour wherein the Son of man cometh**" (Matt. 25:1-13).

36. "Cast me not away from thy presence; and take not thy holy spirit from me" (Ps. 51:11).

(This indicates that the Holy Spirit could be removed from people.)

37. "For the people turneth not unto him that smiteth them, neither do they seek the Lord of hosts" (Isa. 9:13).

(The tribulation period will be that way. We already see lots of people like this today who do not turn to God even during hardships.)

38. "And take heed to yourselves, lest at any time your hearts be overcharged with surfeiting, and drunkenness, and **cares of this life,** and *so* **that day come upon you unawares. For as a snare shall it come on all them that dwell on the face of the whole earth. Watch ye therefore, and pray always, that ye may be ac-**

counted worthy to escape all these things that shall come to pass, and to stand before the Son of man" (Luke 21:34-36).

39. "And he said unto them, Ye are they which justify your-selves before men; but God knoweth your hearts: for **that which is highly esteemed among men is abomination in the sight of God**" (Luke 16:15).

(We need to be careful what we choose to believe is right and true to God.)

40. "Behold, **I come as a thief.** Blessed *is* he that watcheth, and keepeth his garments, lest he walk naked, and they see his shame" (Rev. 16:15).

(We should not want to lose our righteousness.)

41. "For we would not, brethren, have you ignorant of our trouble which came to us in Asia, that we were pressed out of measure, above strength, insomuch that we despaired even of life: But **we had the sentence of death in ourselves, that we should not trust in ourselves, but in God which raiseth the dead**" (2 Cor. 1:8-9).

(When you suffer similarly, put your trust in the Lord, not yourself.)

42. "That ye be not soon shaken in mind, or be troubled, neither by spirit, nor by word, nor by letter as from us, as that **the day of Christ** is at hand. Let no man deceive you by any means: for *that day shall not come*, **except there come a falling away first, and that man of sin be revealed, the son of perdition; Who opposeth and exalteth himself above all that is called God,** or that is worshipped; **so that he as God sitteth in the temple of God, shewing himself that he is God**" (2 Thess. 2:2-4).

(Here we see that the antichrist is to come and claim to be God before Christ returns for us. He is the antichrist, not God. How many Christians would fall away from their pastors, church, and faith if they discovered their pastors were wrong about a rapture occurring at the beginning of the seven year tribulation period and found themselves going through the tribulation period?)

43. "But when ye shall see the abomination of desolation, spoken of by Daniel the prophet, standing where it ought not, (let him that readeth understand,) then let them that be *in* Judaea flee to the mountains: And let him that is on the housetop not go down into the house, neither enter *therein*, to take any thing out of his house: And let him that is in the field not turn back again for to take up his garment.

"But woe to them that are with child, and to them that give suck in those days! And pray ye that your flight be not in the winter. For in those days shall be affliction, such as was not from the beginning of the creation which God created unto this time, neither shall be. And except that the Lord had shortened those days, no flesh should be saved: but for **the elect's sake, whom he hath chosen,** he hath shortened the days.

"And then if any man shall say to you, Lo, here *is* Christ; or, lo, *he* is there; believe *him* not: For false Christs and false prophets shall rise, and shall shew signs and wonders, to seduce, if *it were* possible, even the elect. But take ye heed: behold, I have foretold you all things.

"But in those days, **after that tribulation, the sun shall be darkened,** and the **moon shall not give her light,** And the **stars of heaven shall fall,** and the powers that are in heaven shall be shaken. And **then shall they see the Son of man coming in the clouds with great power and glory.**

"And then shall he send his angels, and shall gather together his elect from the four winds, from the uttermost part of the earth to the uttermost part of heaven. Now learn a parable of the fig tree; When her branch is yet tender, and putteth forth leaves, ye know that summer is near: So ye in like manner, when ye shall see these things come to pass, know that it is nigh, *even* at the doors.

"Verily I say unto you, that this **generation** shall not pass, till all these things be done. Heaven and earth shall pass away: but my words shall not pass away. But of that day and *that* hour knoweth no man, no, not the angels which are in heaven, neither the Son, but the Father. **Take ye heed, watch** and **pray**: for ye know not when the time is" (Mark 13:14-33).

(*Strong's Greek Dictionary* 1074 means **generation**, age, nation, and time.)

44. "But this is that which was spoken by the prophet Joel; And it shall come to pass in the last days, saith God, I will pour out of my Spirit upon all flesh: and your sons and your daughters shall prophesy, and your young men shall see visions, and your old men shall dream dreams: And on my servants and on my handmaidens I will pour out in those days of my Spirit; and they shall prophesy: And **I will shew wonders in heaven above, and signs in the earth** beneath; **blood**, and **fire**, and **vapour of smoke: The sun shall be turned into darkness, and the moon into blood, before that great and notable day of the Lord come:** And it shall come to pass, *that* whosoever shall call on the name of the Lord shall be saved" (Acts 2:16-21).

45. "And I looked, and behold a white cloud, and upon the cloud *one* sat like unto the Son of man, having on his head a golden crown, and in his hand a sharp sickle. And another angel came out of the temple, crying with a loud voice to him that sat on the cloud, **Thrust in thy sickle, and reap:** for the time is come for thee to reap; for the harvest of the earth is ripe. And he that sat on the cloud thrust in his sickle on the earth; **and the earth was reaped.**

"And another angel came out of the temple which is in heaven, he also having a sharp sickle. And another angel came out from the altar, which had power over fire; and cried with a loud cry to him that had the sharp sickle, saying, **Thrust in thy sharp sickle, and gather the clusters of the vine of the earth; for her grapes are fully ripe. And the angel thrust in his sickle into the earth, and gathered the vine of the earth, and cast** *it* **into the great winepress of the wrath of God**" (Rev. 14:14-19).

(The wrath of God is for the lost.)

46. "Behold, I shew you **a mystery; We shall not all sleep, but we shall all be changed, In** a moment, in the twinkling of an eye, **at the last trump: for the trumpet shall sound, and the dead shall be raised incorruptible, and we shall be changed**" (1 Cor. 15:51-52).

(That tells us that Jesus Christ returns at the last trump. The last trump I see listed is in Rev. 11:15 when the seventh angel sounds his trumpet.)

47. "For this corruptible must put on incorruption, and this mortal *must* put on immortality. So **when this corruptible shall have put on incorruption, and this mortal shall have put on immortality, then shall be brought to pass the saying that is written, Death is swallowed up in victory**" (1 Cor. 15:53-54).

(The following paragraph is taken from a previous manuscript I wrote.)

"Significance of the Shofar: The Shout of God's Victory" states that **the last trump** was sometimes referred to as the trump in Rosh Hashanah on the first day of Tishri and that the trumpet blast on Yom Kippur was referred to as **the great trump** (Parsons, John J., 2009, <www.hebrew4christians.com/ Holidays/Fall_Holidays/Elul/Shofar/shofar.html>). Tishri corresponds somewhat with October. With that seventh trumpet eventually comes forth the third woe (Rev. 11:14), God's wrath

(Rev. 11:18) which is brought forth in seven vials by seven angels (Rev. 15:1, 7; 16:1-21).

(Rosh Hashanah is the Feast of Trumpets; Yom Kippur is the Day of Atonement)

48. "And then shall appear the sign of the Son of man in heaven: and then shall all the tribes of the earth mourn, and they shall **see** the **Son of man coming in the clouds** of heaven with power and great glory. And he shall send his angels with a **great sound of a trumpet,** and they shall gather together his elect from the four winds, from one end of heaven to the other" (Matt. 24:30-31).

49. "And the **seventh angel sounded;** and there were great voices in heaven, saying, **The kingdoms of this world are become** *the kingdoms* **of our Lord, and of his Christ; and he shall reign for ever and ever.** And the four and twenty elders, which sat before God on their seats, fell upon their faces, and worshipped God, Saying, We give thee thanks, O Lord God Almighty, which art, and wast, and art to come; because thou hast taken to thee thy great power, and hast reigned.

"And the **nations were angry,** and **thy wrath is come,** and **the time of the dead, that they should be judged,** and that thou shouldest give reward unto thy servants the prophets, and to the saints, and them that fear thy name, small and great; and shouldest destroy them which destroy the earth. And the temple of God was opened in heaven, and there was seen in his temple the ark of his testament: and there were **lightnings,** and **voices,** and **thunderings,** and an **earthquake,** and **great hail**" (Rev. 11:15-19).

(The seventh trumpet sounded. If death is swallowed up in victory at a "rapture" before the seven-year period containing the great tribulation period, then what happens to the believers found within the book of Revelation period?)

50. "But now is Christ risen from the dead, *and* become the firstfruits of them that slept. For since by man *came* death, by man *came* also the resurrection of the dead. For as in Adam all die, even so in Christ shall all be made alive. But **every man in his own order: Christ the firstfruits; afterward they that are Christ's at his coming.** Then *cometh* the end, when he shall have delivered up the kingdom to God, even the Father; when he shall have put down all rule and all authority and power. For he must reign, till he hath put all enemies under his feet" (1 Cor. 15:20-25).

51. "And this is the Father's will which hath sent me, that of all which he hath given me I should lose nothing, but should raise it up again **at the last day.** And this is the will of him that sent me, that every one which seeth the Son, and believeth on him, may have everlasting life: and I will raise him up **at the last day**" (John 6:39-40).

Perhaps this chapter has caused some of us to reconsider what the future will be for Christians. There is to be a catching up of Christians at the time of Jesus' return. Have any of us seen proof that the catching up is to actually be at the beginning of the seven year tribulation period? What I have seen is quite different. It is best for each of us to clearly hear from God ourselves.

VI

PREPARE FOR TODAY

Lots of people probably remember the story of the three little pigs. Each one built a house. The first used straw. The big bad wolf blew it down, so he scurried to his brother's house.

That brother pig had built his house of sticks. The wolf arrived there and blew it down, so both little pigs scrambled to the third brother pig's house. This brother had wisdom. He had built his house of bricks. The wolf could not destroy it, so their lives were saved.

The wolf story is a fairy tale, but our adversary, the devil, has had thousands of years to seek after and destroy millions of people with his lies. Are we certain of our salvation?

"And if the **righteous scarcely be saved,** where shall the ungodly and the sinner appear?" (1 Pet. 4:18). There are some things we should begin to do now. Of course, repentance and salvation are needed first.

We need to ask Jesus Christ to forgive us of our sins and save us. Ask Him for the baptism of the Holy Ghost, also known as the Holy Spirit.

Before the outpouring of the Holy Ghost occurred, Jesus had told His disciples that they would be baptized with the Holy Spirit (Acts 1:5). After that pronouncement, Jesus made a very profound statement. "But ye shall receive power, after that the Holy Ghost is come **upon** you: and ye shall be witnesses unto me both in Jerusalem, and in all Judaea, and in Samaria, and unto the uttermost part of the earth" (Acts 1:8).

Being baptized with the Holy Ghost was when the Holy Ghost would come **upon** the disciples. They would then become witnesses for Jesus throughout the earth. Even after Jesus was baptized in water, the Holy Ghost came down **upon** Him. He is our prime example to imitate.

Later in Ephesus, Paul found some disciples of John the Baptist who had not even heard of the Holy Ghost (Acts 19:2). Paul enlightened them.

> *Then said Paul, John verily baptized with the baptism of repentance, saying unto the people, that they should believe on him which should come after him, that is, on Christ Jesus. When they heard this, they were baptized in the name of the Lord Jesus* (Acts 19:4-5).

After they were then baptized in water, Paul laid his hands on them, the Holy Ghost came **upon** those people, and they began to speak in tongues and prophesy. "And when Paul had laid his hands upon them, the Holy Ghost came on them; and they spake with tongues, and prophesied" (Acts 19:6).

Whoever has not been baptized in water should get it done. Then let a true man or woman of God lay hands on them so that the Holy Ghost will come upon them, and they can expect to speak in tongues and prophesy.

Christians are to be equipped with spiritual armor.

> *Wherefore take unto you the whole armour of God, that ye may be able to withstand in the evil day, and having done all, to stand. Stand therefore, having your loins girt about with truth, and having on the breastplate of righteousness; And your feet shod with the preparation of the gospel of peace; Above all, taking the shield of faith, wherewith ye shall be able to quench all the fiery darts of the wicked. And take the helmet of salva-*

*tion, and the sword of the Spirit, which is the word of God:
Praying always with all prayer and supplication in the Spirit,
and watching thereunto with all perseverance and supplication
for all saints* (Eph. 6:13-18).

Notice that it is a command to take the armor unto ourselves. Jesus Christ is both truth and the Word of God.

Do we read God's Word, or do we decorate our coffee tables with it? Do we live righteously, or do we follow the lusts of the flesh and eyes and the pride of life? Do we walk in the peace God has given us, or do we cause strife, division, and contention?

Do we live and walk in faith daily, or do we just carry our faith when we attend a church meeting? Do we guard our mind from the assaults against the realization of our salvation, or do we let thoughts of doubt erode away traces of our knowledge of the truth of our salvation?

Do we carry in our mind scripture that we have memorized, or do we just carry a paper or electronic copy of the Word of God, which is the sword of the Spirit? Do we pray always for all the saints (Christians), or do we neglect our responsibility to do so?

Another very important scripture should be adhered to by every Christian:

*And be not conformed to this world: but be ye transformed by
the renewing of your mind, that ye may prove what is that
good, and acceptable, and perfect, will of God. For I say,
through the grace given unto me, to every man that is among
you, not to think of himself more highly than he ought to think;
but to think soberly, according as God hath dealt to every man
the measure of faith* (Rom. 12:2-3).

The enemy attacks our minds a lot. The devil spoke to Jesus, so we can expect some devils to speak to us at times. We may not realize that an enemy is speaking to us, but if a thought enters our minds to do something foolish, evil, or needlessly dangerous, we should beware. It probably is a devil speaking to us.

Christians have authority over evil thoughts and over devils.

For the weapons of our warfare are not carnal, but mighty through God to the pulling down of strong holds;) Casting down imaginations, and every high thing that exalteth itself against the knowledge of God, and bringing into captivity every thought to the obedience of Christ (2 Cor. 10:4-5).

It is our responsibility to guard our minds. We need to speak out loud to those ungodly thoughts and everything that exalts itself against Christ Jesus, and that includes evil spirits. We need to cast them down. Some evil spirits may even need to be cast out.

And let us consider one another to provoke unto love and to good works: Not forsaking the assembling of ourselves together, as the manner of some is; but exhorting one another: and so much the more, as ye see the day approaching (Heb. 10:24-25).

We are to join together with other Christians so that we can build one another up spiritually.

"He that loveth his life shall lose it; and he that hateth his life in this world shall keep it unto life eternal" (John 12:25). Love and forgiveness must be very prevalent throughout our lives.

Please remember the following extremely important scripture:

We know that we have passed from death unto life, because we love the brethren. He that loveth not his brother abideth in death. Whosoever hateth his brother is a murderer: and ye know that no murderer hath eternal life abiding in him. Hereby perceive we the love of God, because he laid down his life for us:

and we ought to lay down our lives for the brethren. But whoso hath this world's good, and seeth his brother have need, and shutteth up his bowels of compassion from him, how dwelleth the love of God in him? (1 John 3:14-17)

If the third little pig had not prepared well and then helped his two brothers, the wolf would have had two pork feasts. Imagine how God would have us to love and help our neighbors. We must become well grounded in the love of God to prepare victoriously against all the onslaughts of our enemy, the devil.

VII

PROVISION FOR TODAY

We had prayed for years to have a third child, a boy. It seemed there was a promise of one, but we never received the expected pregnancy. One day, an amazing thing seemed to be flung into my wife's path. At a conference, a lady approached my wife and told her about a little boy who had been brought to America for about a month. The boy was one of five out of twenty-two Chinese orphans who had not been adopted. My wife told me of the encounter and let it drop.

I thought about that for two days. What she did not tell me was that she had left it up to the Lord to move upon me to bring up the suggestion of our adopting the boy.

Two days passed when I brought up the possibility of adopting. She sent in our pre-adoption application on a Monday evening. It usually takes at least a week to receive a response from China, but we heard the next day! It usually takes at least a year, and sometimes a year-and-a-half, to complete an adoption. Our efforts were completed in eleven months!

"God looked down from heaven upon the children of men, to see if there were *any* that did understand, that did seek God" (Ps. 53:2). Most people are so concerned today with the cares of the world that they do not spend any time seeking the only living God.

God is still merciful even to those who do not seek Him (Matt. 5:45), though those who refuse to believe in and obey

Him will surely perish. God has promised to care for His beloved children, though it is appointed for men to die once (Heb. 9:27).

"Where *there is* no vision, the people perish: but he that keepeth the law, happy *is* he" (Prov. 29:18). That word "vision" comes from a word that means "sight" or "revelation" (*Strong's Hebrew Dictionary*).

People who do not perceive who God is lack spiritual vision because they are spiritually dead. Cares of the world are one of the things Jesus warned about that distract people from the Word of God and lead people to perish. "And the cares of this world, and the deceitfulness of riches, and the lusts of other things entering in, choke the word, and it becometh unfruitful" (Mark 4:19).

God gave an extremely important warning for all mankind. "My people are destroyed for lack of knowledge: because thou hast rejected knowledge, I will also reject thee, that thou shalt be no priest to me: seeing thou hast forgotten the law of thy God, I will also forget thy children" (Hos. 4:6). All people should seek knowledge of God. Those who do not will surely perish.

In these end times, it is still vitally important for people to seek God. Even the righteous experience persecution, tribulation, and suffering. Many people worry about how they will pay their debts and continue to survive. That is not how God wants people to live.

Jesus Christ gives His believers His peace and joy. When King David grew old, he wrote a verse that believers can take into their own hearts. "I have been young, and *now* am old; yet have I not seen the righteous forsaken, nor his seed begging bread" (Ps. 37:25). We may wonder if that still holds true for today, even if we already know that God remains the same today as always.

But seek ye first the kingdom of God, and his righteousness; and all these things shall be added unto you. Take therefore no thought for the morrow: for the morrow shall take thought for the things of itself. Sufficient unto the day is the evil thereof (Matt. 6:33-34).

We are to notice the stipulation in that scripture. We are to seek God's kingdom and righteousness first; then our needs will be provided for us. The kingdom of God is to be found within us (Luke 17:21) after we accept Jesus Christ into our lives. One may ask what the kingdom of God is. "For the kingdom of God is not meat and drink; but righteousness, and peace, and joy in the Holy Ghost" (Rom. 14:17).

Look at some scriptures regarding seeking God. "The meek shall eat and be satisfied: they shall praise the Lord that seek him: your heart shall live for ever" (Ps. 22:26). If we haven't praised God, it may be that we haven't sought Him.

"The young lions do lack, and suffer hunger: but they that seek the Lord shall not want any good *thing*" (Ps. 34:10). "Seek the Lord, and his strength: seek his face evermore" (Ps. 105:4). "Therefore came I forth to meet thee, diligently to seek thy face, and I have found thee" (Prov. 7:15).

I love them that love me; and those that seek me early shall find me. Riches and honour are with me; yea, durable riches and righteousness. My fruit is better than gold, yea, than fine gold; and my revenue than choice silver (Prov. 8:17-19).

"Evil men understand not judgment: but they that seek the Lord understand all *things*" (Prov. 28:5). "Seek ye the Lord, all ye meek of the earth, which have wrought his judgment; seek righteousness, seek meekness: it may be ye shall be hid in the day of the Lord's anger" (Zeph. 2:3).

Ask, and it shall be given you; seek, and ye shall find; knock, and it shall be opened unto you: For every one that asketh receiveth; and he that seeketh findeth; and to him that knocketh it shall be opened (Matt. 7:7-8).

And seek not ye what ye shall eat, or what ye shall drink, neither be ye of doubtful mind. For all these things do the nations of the world seek after: and your Father knoweth that ye have need of these things. But rather seek ye the kingdom of God; and all these things shall be added unto you (Luke 12:29-31).

Be warned. There were some people who sought Jesus simply because He provided natural food for them. "Jesus answered them and said, Verily, verily, I say unto you, Ye seek me, not because ye saw the miracles, but because ye did eat of the loaves, and were filled" (John 6:26).

If we are thinking that we can just seek Jesus during hard times in order to get natural food, then our seeking would be in vain because we would not be seeking the kingdom of God first nor His righteousness.

"For whosoever will save his life shall lose it; but whosoever shall lose his life for my sake and the gospel's, the same shall save it. For what shall it profit a man, if he shall gain the whole world, and lose his own soul?" (Mark 8:35-36). "But whosoever shall deny me before men, him will I also deny before my Father which is in heaven" (Matt. 10:33). "And having food and raiment let us be therewith content" (1 Tim. 6:8).

Trust in the Lord, and do good; so shalt thou dwell in the land, and verily thou shalt be fed. Delight thyself also in the Lord; and he shall give thee the desires of thine heart. Commit thy way unto the Lord; trust also in him; and he shall bring it to pass. And he shall bring forth thy righteousness as the light, and thy judgment as the noonday (Ps. 37:3-6).

Remember the former things of old: for I am God, and there is none else; I am God, and there is none like me, Declaring the end from the beginning, and from ancient times the things that are not yet done, saying, My counsel shall stand, and I will do all my pleasure (Isa. 46:9-10).

God created each of us for His good pleasure (Rev. 4:11). Someone asked if God could create a rock so big that He could not pick it up. First of all, God is not foolish as some people may think. He already created all things that are created, so someone could ask the persons who ask that foolish question just how big that rock would have to be?

"Answer not a fool according to his folly, lest thou also be like unto him. Answer a fool according to his folly, lest he be wise in his own conceit" (Prov. 26:4-5). We have two choices. If we answer a fool according to his folly, we may prevent him from being wise in his own conceit. However, if we answer the fool, there is danger we could become like him!

We can ask foolish people if God could die and live again. We know Jesus Christ has already accomplished that for us.

The point is that during each day we live, we have to put our trust in our loving God. We don't know exactly when we are to die, but God knows. He also knows who will be part of the privileged believers who are alive at the second coming of Jesus Christ.

He knew before the beginning of creation what was going to happen to each of us. See what God knew about a set of twins:

And not only this; but when Rebecca also had conceived by one, even by our father Isaac; (For the children being not yet born, neither having done any good or evil, that the purpose of God according to election might stand, not of works, but of him that calleth;) It was said unto her, The elder shall serve the younger.

As it is written, Jacob have I loved, but Esau have I hated (Rom. 9:10-13).

God knows each of our needs. He even has the hairs of our heads numbered (Matt. 10:30; Luke 12:7). He can look into our hearts to see what we treasure. "For where your treasure is, there will your heart be also" (Matt. 6:21).

Man's life is in his blood. "When he maketh inquisition for blood, he remembereth them: he forgetteth not the cry of the humble" (Ps. 9:12).

For he shall deliver the needy when he crieth; the poor also, and him that hath no helper. He shall spare the poor and needy, and shall save the souls of the needy. He shall redeem their soul from deceit and violence: and precious shall their blood be in his sight (Ps. 72:12-14).

We must remain humble and keep seeking after God and His righteousness. We need to honor Jesus Christ first and foremost in our lives and train our children to do likewise.

We can watch for Jesus Christ daily and maintain our faith always, even in the worst of times, in order to remain faithful to Him. We are not our own. "What? know ye not that your body is the temple of the Holy Ghost *which* is in you, which ye have of God, and ye are not your own? For ye are bought with a price: therefore glorify God in your body, and in your spirit, which are God's" (1 Cor. 6:19-20).

"Examine yourselves, whether ye be in the faith; prove your own selves. Know ye not your own selves, how that Jesus Christ is in you, except ye be reprobates?" (2 Cor. 13:5). God loves His people, but it is our own responsibility to remain faithful to Him.

We don't always know how God will provide for us, but we can still trust Him moment by moment. As we found out about the third child we desired, we discovered God had a way we had not really investigated. I think God likes to surprise us sometimes with His wonders and care.

VIII

WORD TO THE WISE

In my search for knowledge and understanding, I came across a book that appeared interesting—*Willmington's Complete Guide to Bible Knowledge*. Harold Willmington expressed the minuteness of man by stating that if the earth was considered the size of a grain of sand, the sun could be represented by an orange thirty feet away. Amazingly, the nearest star would be over a thousand miles from the orange-sized sun.

Other fascinating comparisons are also illustrated. Even our sun is small. We are little people, regardless of how great we may think we are. It behooves us to remember just how small we are in comparison to God who created and owns us.

Sometimes man thinks of himself as very important. However, when we view man from God's perspective, it can be shocking. "Behold, the nations are as a drop of a bucket, and are counted as the small dust of the balance: behold, he taketh up the isles as a very little thing" (Isa. 40:15).

Even those who think they are safely saved should pay close attention to God's Word. Some people who think they are correct in their thinking are actually wrong. "Every way of a man *is* right in his own eyes: but the Lord pondereth the hearts" (Prov. 21:2).

All people need to make positively sure that they are not speaking against or fighting against God. What is coming before Christ's return will stagger the imagination of many people, even believers.

Pay attention to the first part of the following scripture.

Let no man deceive you by any means: for that day shall not come, except there come a falling away first, and that man of sin be revealed, the son of perdition; Who opposeth and exalteth himself above all that is called God, or that is worshipped; so that he as God sitteth in the temple of God, shewing himself that he is God (2 Thess. 2:3-4).

There is coming a falling away from the faith by many people. You may ask how that could be. There is a difference between knowing about Jesus Christ and actually knowing Him. A true believer will know Him personally.

Knowing Him will involve a two-way communication between the true believer and the living Christ Jesus. "I am the good shepherd, and know my sheep, and am known of mine" (John 10:14). "My sheep hear my voice, and I know them, and they follow me: And I give unto them eternal life; and they shall never perish, neither shall any *man* pluck them out of my hand" (John 10:27-28). Do you hear Jesus' voice? Do you follow Him?

Some people believe that they are guaranteed salvation because they have joined a particular denomination. I have never read any scripture indicating that to be true.

However, when Jesus was crucified, there was one thief on a cross who was promised to be in paradise with Jesus. That thief did not join any church to get saved.

Some people may think they are saved because they had an ancestor who had faith in God; or a person may have faith in his or her spouse's faith. That does not save a person. Faith must be in Jesus Christ, the shedding of His blood, and His sacrificial death on the cross.

The above examples are of people who are not saved but may think that they are. However, the falling away refers to true believers falling away from the faith. Many people claim that once a person becomes a Christian, then that person will always be a Christian. That is a false belief, a false doctrine.

Beware of false doctrines. God has declared that some believers will fall away. Who are we to believe is correct, God or mere man? Only those who remain faithful to Jesus Christ unto the end will always be considered Christian.

Another serious situation has also been addressed in scripture. There will be people who think that they are saved but will discover differently in the judgment.

Strive to enter in at the strait gate: for many, I say unto you, will seek to enter in, and shall not be able. When once the master of the house is risen up, and hath shut to the door, and ye begin to stand without, and to knock at the door, saying, Lord, Lord, open unto us; and he shall answer and say unto you, I know you not whence ye are: Then shall ye begin to say, We have eaten and drunk in thy presence, and thou hast taught in our streets. But he shall say, I tell you, I know you not whence ye are; depart from me, all ye workers of iniquity (Luke 13:24-27).

Not every one that saith unto me, Lord, Lord, shall enter into the kingdom of heaven; but he that doeth the will of my Father which is in heaven. Many will say to me in that day, Lord, Lord, have we not prophesied in thy name? and in thy name have cast out devils? and in thy name done many wonderful works? And then will I profess unto them, I never knew you: depart from me, ye that work iniquity (Matt. 7:21-23).

It will be too late for those people to repent. They will have lived their lives foolishly. True believers will be doers of the Word of God and not just hearers of it. Good works must follow a person's faith. Otherwise, that person's faith is worthless, and they are what scripture calls dead works.

Here is a very crucial scripture many Christians possibly have forgotten. "And if the righteous scarcely be saved, where shall the ungodly and the sinner appear?" (1 Pet. 4:18). How secure is our salvation right now? Have we ever talked to God about it?

Have we heard or read what some people will be like in the end times?

> *This know also, that in the last days perilous times shall come. For men shall be lovers of their own selves, covetous, boasters, proud, blasphemers, disobedient to parents, unthankful, unholy, Without natural affection, trucebreakers, false accusers, incontinent, fierce, despisers of those that are good, Traitors, heady, highminded, lovers of pleasures more than lovers of God; Having a form of godliness, but denying the power thereof: from such turn away. For of this sort are they which creep into houses, and lead captive silly women laden with sins, led away with divers lusts, Ever learning, and never able to come to the knowledge of the truth. Now as Jannes and Jambres withstood Moses, so do these also resist the truth: men of corrupt minds, reprobate concerning the faith. But they shall proceed no further: for their folly shall be manifest unto all men, as theirs also was* (2 Tim. 3:1-9).

> *Beloved, when I gave all diligence to write unto you of the common salvation, it was needful for me to write unto you, and exhort you that ye should earnestly contend for the faith which was once delivered unto the saints. For there are certain men crept in unawares, who were before of old ordained to this condemnation, ungodly men, turning the grace of our God into lasciviousness, and denying the only Lord God, and our Lord Jesus Christ* (Jude 1:3-4).

Would we rather be those who earnestly contend for the faith or those ordained to condemnation? Continue to read and consider how safe we should be in our faith.

The Lord knoweth how to deliver the godly out of temptations, and to reserve the unjust unto the day of judgment to be punished: But chiefly them that walk after the flesh in the lust of uncleanness, and despise government. Presumptuous are they, selfwilled, they are not afraid to speak evil of dignities.

Whereas angels, which are greater in power and might, bring not railing accusation against them before the Lord.

But these, as natural brute beasts, made to be taken and destroyed, speak evil of the things that they understand not; and shall utterly perish in their own corruption; And shall receive the reward of unrighteousness, as they that count it pleasure to riot in the day time. Spots they are and blemishes, sporting themselves with their own deceivings while they feast with you;

Having eyes full of adultery, and that cannot cease from sin; beguiling unstable souls: an heart they have exercised with covetous practices; cursed children:

Which have forsaken the right way, and are gone astray, following the way of Balaam the son of Bosor, who loved the wages of unrighteousness; But was rebuked for his iniquity: the dumb ass speaking with man's voice forbad the madness of the prophet.

These are wells without water, clouds that are carried with a tempest; to whom the mist of darkness is reserved for ever. For when they speak great swelling words of vanity, they allure through the lusts of the flesh, through much wantonness, those that were clean escaped from them who live in error.

While they promise them liberty, they themselves are the servants of corruption: for of whom a man is overcome, of the same is he brought in bondage. For if after they have escaped the pollutions of the world through the knowledge of the Lord and Saviour Jesus Christ, they are again entangled therein, and overcome, the latter end is worse with them than the beginning.

For it had been better for them not to have known the way of righteousness, than, after they have known it, to turn from the holy commandment delivered unto them. But it is happened unto them according to the true proverb, The dog is turned to his own vomit again; and the sow that was washed to her wallowing in the mire (2 Pet. 2:9-22).

This is a critical time in history because we are already living in the end times. That scripture mentioned that some people could have known the way of righteousness but then turned away from it. It also states that their latter end would be even worse than before they had become believers.

Have you heard the lie that a person cannot lose his or her salvation?

Thus saith the Lord; Cursed be the man that trusteth in man, and maketh flesh his arm, and whose heart departeth from the Lord. For he shall be like the heath in the desert, and shall not see when good cometh; but shall inhabit the parched places in the wilderness, in a salt land and not inhabited (Jer. 17:5-6).

Are we willing to rely on mere man's word or God's Word? Today is the day of decision for us. Establish a real relationship with the living God in and through Jesus Christ. We need Jesus as our best friend. We need to allow Him to speak into our lives. Learn to hear and discern His voice. God's Word tells us to be still and know that He is God (Ps. 46:10).

After learning how minute humans are, it seems a wonder that God even created us, let alone created us in His own image. We are truly blessed to be humans. A third of the angels rebelled and decided to follow a false leader, the devil. They were evicted from heaven and do not have a chance to repent. Their end will be in the lake of fire for eternity. We have a chance to either believe God and submit to Him or forfeit everything and join the fallen angels for eternity in that lake of fire.

That is why choosing to believe in Jesus Christ is of immediate importance. None of us knows when we will depart from our mortal lives. We cannot just trust in our own earthly wisdom. Who are we to deny the existence of the living God?

IX

CHECK YOUR FAITH

There was a young fellow who did not always brush his teeth when needed. Even when his parents told him to do it, he sometimes put it off. I know the boy's dad. He relayed an unusual story to me.

When his son failed to brush his teeth one particular time, the dad had to become resourceful because he did not want his son to suffer tooth decay and possibly infections or loss of teeth. This dad had to show love to his son but make a strong point to get his son to obey. I don't know where he came up with his scheme.

After the son admitted that he had not brushed his teeth again, the dad put his plan into action. He went to the bathroom, picked up a toilet bowl cleaning brush, and went to confront his son. He gave his son one more chance to brush his teeth, or else his dad was going to brush them for him with the toilet brush. The son finally got the message that his father meant what he said.

Ask God for understanding of His Word. "You have not because you ask not" (Jas. 4:2). If we want to know God is real, we need to learn to hear His voice. When we learn to hear and discern His voice, we will be greatly encouraged in our faith. Also, we will be able to ask God questions and listen for His answers.

People in the Bible are examples for our lives, primarily to avoid mistakes such as they made and to learn to follow after righteousness. One of the greatest books of the Bible to study is Judges.

Observe the following two verses. "And the people served the Lord all the days of Joshua, and all the days of the elders that outlived Joshua, who had seen all the great works of the Lord, that he did for Israel" (Judg. 2:7). "And also all that generation were gathered unto their fathers: and there arose another generation after them, which knew not the Lord, nor yet the works which he had done for Israel" (Judg. 2:10).

The generation that saw the great works of God had served the Lord, but the next generation had not learned to know Him and did not know of the great works that He had done for Israel. The previous generation had not trained up the next generation to know the Lord or about His works.

That is much the same today, but ignorance doesn't release us from responsibility. "And, ye fathers, provoke not your children to wrath: but bring them up in the nurture and admonition of the Lord" (Eph. 6:4).

A horrible pattern was exhibited by Israel throughout the book of Judges. When a leader was raised up, often the people would follow his or her leading. However, when a leader died, the people often turned to worshipping false gods and forsook the Lord. Then the anger of the Lord was against Israel.

His anger did not arise against them just because their leader had died. It was because they turned against Him and worshipped false gods. That is what people should be aware of today. We are not to turn away from God just because a godly leader dies.

However, the United States has gone woefully wrong, not just because of the errors of the government, but also because many of the people have been ignorant of the true God. They do not realize that He does bring judgment upon people and nations although He does not want anyone to perish.

Sin is sin even for unbelievers. "Then when lust hath conceived, it bringeth forth sin: and sin, when it is finished, bringeth forth death" (Jas. 1:15). People often don't cry out to God unless they suffer extreme illness, injury, emotional grief, or financial loss. Other factors may be natural disasters or national disasters such as the attack against the twin towers in New York.

It seems the duration of the extreme suffering or loss usually has to be a considerably long period of time before people will truly seek after God. We must be doers of God's Word (Jas. 1:22). Otherwise, we deceive ourselves.

> *Every tree that bringeth not forth good fruit is hewn down, and cast into the fire. Wherefore by their fruits ye shall know them. Not every one that saith unto me, Lord, Lord, shall enter into the kingdom of heaven; but he that doeth the will of my Father which is in heaven. Many will say to me in that day, Lord, Lord, have we not prophesied in thy name? and in thy name have cast out devils? and in thy name done many wonderful works? And then will I profess unto them, I never knew you: depart from me, ye that work iniquity* (Matt. 7:19-23).

Being a doer of God's Word includes opposing promiscuity, homosexuality, fornication, adultery, transsexuality, transvestism, and abortion in addition to all other sins. A person can repent of such sins and put faith in Jesus Christ to be saved, but how can anyone accept Jesus Christ and then live in support of such evil? Those who do not trust the Lord may be easily swayed or seduced into such sins, so beware.

Read chapters twenty-seven and twenty-eight of Deuteronomy to learn about God's view of our lives and what actions will bring curses upon us. Those chapters are very important, so we must not fail ourselves or our families by disregarding that advice. "As the bird by wandering, as the swallow by flying, so the curse causeless shall not come" (Prov. 26:2).

Many false doctrines are being preached today. Do we know the Bible well enough to protect ourselves and our families from the lies? God has graciously informed mankind about how to discern the true spirits from the false.

*Beloved, believe not every spirit, but try the spirits whether they are of God: because many false prophets are gone out into the world. Hereby know ye the Spirit of God: Every spirit that confesseth that **Jesus Christ** is come in the flesh is of God: And every spirit that confesseth not that **Jesus Christ** is come in the flesh is not of God: and this is that spirit of antichrist, whereof ye have heard that it should come; and even now already is it in the world* (1 John 4:1-3).

We will have no excuse on judgment day for not guarding ourselves now. It is our responsibility. "Study to shew thyself approved unto God, a workman that needeth not to be ashamed, rightly dividing the word of truth" (2 Tim. 2:15). Just because we have free will and are adults does not excuse us from obeying God. He does not want us to perish, but specific requirements have been presented by God that one must obey in order to receive eternal life.

Because of the following truth, there is great danger to every person: "Every way of a man is right in his own eyes: but the Lord pondereth the hearts" (Prov. 21:2). That verse alone should give every person reason enough to realize that we need to read God's Word in order to discover His truth and be able to escape self-deceptive thoughts.

"A wise *man* feareth, and departeth from evil: but the fool rageth, and is confident" (Prov. 14:16). We are told to put on the mind of Christ and be transformed by the renewing of our minds. We should renew our minds by reading and studying God's Word.

Spiritual lukewarmness is extremely dangerous. Jesus Christ warned the Laodicean church of that in Revelation.

And unto the angel of the church of the Laodiceans write; These things saith the Amen, the faithful and true witness, the beginning of the creation of God; I know thy works, that thou art neither cold nor hot: I would thou wert cold or hot. So then because thou art lukewarm, and neither cold nor hot, I will spue thee out of my mouth.

Because thou sayest, I am rich, and increased with goods, and have need of nothing; and knowest not that thou art wretched, and miserable, and poor, and blind, and naked: I counsel thee to buy of me gold tried in the fire, that thou mayest be rich; and white raiment, that thou mayest be clothed, and that the shame of thy nakedness do not appear; and anoint thine eyes with eyesalve, that thou mayest see (Rev. 3:14-18).

If we become naked spiritually, then we would no longer have robes of righteousness. Being blind in that scripture refers to being spiritually blind.

In other words, the people in that church were at a tipping point of either repenting or else facing eternal death in the lake of fire where their spirits would suffer endless torment. Are we spiritually hot, lukewarm, or cold? Are we growing in the knowledge of the Lord Jesus and maturing spiritually?

Are we helping the poor, the orphans, and the widows (who are at least sixty years old without family to help them in their needs) especially financially? I don't mean supporting rip-off artists panhandling. We should help those who are truly poor so God will help us when we have needs.

If a husband does not treat his wife right, his prayers will not be answered. "Likewise, ye husbands, dwell with *them* according to knowledge, giving honour unto the wife, as unto the weaker vessel, and as being heirs together of the grace of life; that your prayers be not hindered" (1 Pet. 3:7).

If we don't know if we are treating our wives correctly, each man should ask his own wife what she thinks about it. If a husband does not provide for his family's needs, then he is worse than an infidel (1 Tim. 5:8).

Scripture also warns us not to make friends with an angry man (Prov. 22:24). "An angry man stirreth up strife, and a furious man aboundeth in transgression" (Prov. 29:22). "*He that is soon angry dealeth foolishly: and a man of wicked devices is hated*" (Prov. 14:17).

Who is the one you put first in your life? Is it your parents, grandparent, your boss, a friend, boy friend, girl friend, person of infatuation, sibling, teacher, pastor, prophet, yourself, or Jesus Christ? "If any man come to me, and hate not his father, and mother, and wife, and children, and brethren, and sisters, yea, and his own life also, he cannot be my disciple" (Luke 14:26). In my understanding, we are to put Jesus even before the people we dearly love.

"He that loveth his life shall lose it; and he that hateth his life in this world shall keep it unto life eternal" (John 12:25). We are to always put Jesus Christ first in all things and all ways. How can we be witnesses for Him if we place someone else first in our hearts before Him?

How can we be witnesses for Him if we reject the true teaching in the Bible that we are to become witnesses for Him after the Holy Spirit comes upon us? "But ye shall receive power, after that the Holy Ghost is come upon you: and ye shall be witnesses unto me both in Jerusalem, and in all Judaea, and in Samaria, and unto the uttermost part of the earth" (Acts 1:8).

Consider where we are spiritually today. Do we seek to know God and His Word, or do we just ignore Him? Do we do anything to try to help win anyone to faith in Jesus Christ? Do we believe everything anyone states from a church pulpit to be true?

Those are serious questions to consider. We may be of the belief that we are headed for heaven, but it could be possible that we are actually still headed for hell. Find out before it is too late! Let's allow God's Word to teach us to fear Him.

"Ye adulterers and adulteresses, know ye not that the friend-ship of the world is enmity with God? whosoever therefore will be a friend of the world is the enemy of God" (Jas. 4:4). The world is quickly approaching a likeness to the days of Noah and those of Lot.

Though Noah was a preacher, only he and his family were saved from the worldwide flood. Seemingly few people attend a true Christian church today, and not all who do are actually saved.

In the day when angels led Lot out of Sodom, homosexu-ality was rampant, and such people violent. Likewise today, many people are ignorant concerning the seriousness of sin, es-pecially the sin of homosexuality.

However, Jesus Christ warned that the world would become like the days of Noah and Lot before His return to earth. If we are waiting for a sign from God before we are willing to repent and put our faith in Jesus Christ, we may soon become even more deceived. One called the antichrist will come forth portraying himself as a wondrous man and then proclaiming himself to be God, deceiving multitudes of people around the world.

Now the Spirit speaketh expressly, that in the latter times some shall depart from the faith, giving heed to seducing spirits, and doctrines of devils; Speaking lies in hypocrisy; having their con-science seared with a hot iron; Forbidding to marry, and com-manding to abstain from meats, which God hath created to be received with thanksgiving of them which believe and know the truth (1 Tim. 4:1-3).

Some shall become so deceived that they shall depart from the faith! "For false Christs and false prophets shall rise, and shall shew signs and wonders, to seduce, if it *were* possible, even the elect" (Mark 13:22).

Our lives and the lives of our children and grandchildren are at stake today. "While it is said, To day if ye will hear his voice, harden not your hearts, as in the provocation" (Heb. 3:15). "Again, he limiteth a certain day, saying in David, To day, after so long a time; as it is said, To day if ye will hear his voice, harden not your hearts" (Heb. 4:7).

We have a choice, a free will choice. Because God has warned us that the deceptions will be so great that even some Christians will fall away from the faith, do we see the extreme danger our lives may be in even now? Because there are even some false ministers, be encouraged to begin to study the Bible to strengthen your faith and train your children with the truth. Learn to hear God's voice so that you will know He is real. "For his anger *endureth but* a moment; in his favour is life: weeping may endure for a night, but joy *cometh* in the morning" (Ps. 30:5). Pick up the Word of God, and let Him show you how much He loves you.

I don't expect God to come after us with a toilet brush to try to get us to respond properly in a timely fashion. However, God's warnings are much more serious regarding our lives. He does not want us or our children to die and go to hell and the lake of fire.

We need to set our priorities so that salvation from sin is a top one, one not to be procrastinated. Since we do not know how long we have yet to live, today is the best day to go to God and His Word.

X

DIFFICULT SCRIPTURE

There was a man who was once enrolled in an advanced math course. He did not understand the information, and he did not read his text book to try to learn it. He may have even gotten a grade of "C" on a test.

He still did not understand or study the book. He probably just looked over his notes before the tests. When the end of the course arrived, he was faced with a final exam. The man wasn't too concerned, probably because he still didn't understand enough of the course information to be too concerned about it. A day or so later, he found out his grade for the whole course. He had failed, so he did not have enough credits to graduate.

Next semester, the man took the same course under a different instructor. The man did not study much that time either, but he did study the notes more carefully before tests. He actually put forth some effort. Wonder of wonders, the man squeaked by with a passing grade, but he still did not understand the material. He had just been able to reproduce on the test what he remembered from his notes, and that is why he was able to pass.

"Be ye therefore perfect, even as your Father which is in heaven is perfect" (Matt. 5:48). Is that possible? How does a person become perfect? Apparently, it is possible.

Consider Job. "And the Lord said unto Satan, Hast thou considered my servant Job, that there is none like him in the earth, a **perfect** and an upright man, one that feareth God, and escheweth evil?" (Job 1:8).

*And the Lord said unto Satan, Hast thou considered my servant Job, that there is none like him in the earth, a **perfect** and an upright man, one that feareth God, and escheweth evil? and still he holdeth fast his integrity, although thou movedst me against him, to destroy him without cause* (Job 2:3).

Job lived long before Jesus was ever birthed in the flesh. Let's look at some scripture to understand man from God's viewpoint, if we can.

And the Lord God commanded the man, saying, Of every tree of the garden thou mayest freely eat: But of the tree of the knowledge of good and evil, thou shalt not eat of it: for in the day that thou eatest thereof thou shalt surely die (Gen. 2:16-17).

God's day is as a thousand years. "But, beloved, be not ignorant of this one thing, that one day is with the Lord as a thousand years, and a thousand years as one day" (2 Pet. 3:8). The Bible records Methuselah as having lived longer than any other mere man, yet he died within the time limit of one of God's days. "And all the days of Methuselah were nine hundred sixty and nine years: and he died" (Gen. 5:27).

All mankind, except for Jesus Christ, has received the sin nature of the first Adam. Jesus has His Father's nature and is sinless. The bodies of all mankind, except Jesus Christ's, have been sinful. However, Jesus willingly became sin for us. "For he hath made him to be sin for us, who knew no sin; that we might be made the righteousness of God in him" (2 Cor. 5:21).

Paul, a mighty apostle, even stated that no good thing was in his flesh. "For I know that in me (that is, in my flesh) dwelleth no good thing: for to will is present with me; but *how* to perform that which is good I find not" (Rom. 7:18).

What about the soul of man? We are to fear Him who can destroy soul and body in hell (Matt. 10:28). Jesus has the keys of both death and hell (Rev. 1:18). People who choose not to follow Jesus go to hell when they die. Scripture tells us there once was a beggar at the gates of a rich man (Luke 16:19-21). After they both had died, the rich man was in torment in hell while Lazarus, the beggar, was in the abode of the righteous dead. The place of torment did not have any water.

The rich man asked Abraham to send Lazarus with some water to cool his tongue. Abraham responded that there was a great chasm between the two areas that could not be crossed. It is interesting to see what God said about the tongue. "And the tongue is a fire, a world of iniquity: so is the tongue among our members, that it defileth the whole body, and setteth on fire the course of nature; and **it is set on fire of hell**" (Jas. 3:6).

Scripture tells us that when Jesus died, He went to hell and preached to the people there and led captivity captive (Ps. 68:18; Eph. 4:8). He led the righteous spirits (with their souls), whose bodies had died, out of the abode of the righteous dead on the earth. The souls and spirits of the righteous were very much alive.

The souls and spirits of the wicked remained in the place of torment. Even though the souls of the wicked can be destroyed in hell, their spirits do not cease to exist. The unrighteous spirits will eventually be cast into the lake of fire, the second death, where their smoke will rise up forever (Rev. 14:9-11). Those spirits never lose consciousness. They will be in torment forever without hope or rest. It is a terrifying thing.

The lake of fire was actually prepared for the devil and his angels. "Then shall he say also unto them on the left hand, Depart from me, ye cursed, into everlasting fire, prepared for the devil and his angels:" (Matt. 25:41). The first man was created from dust from the earth, but he did not live until the spirit of man originated from the breath of God (Gen. 2:7). Jesus Christ owns all mankind (1 Cor. 6:20; 7:23). So, God is the One who can destroy body and soul in hell.

That brings us to the point in scripture where we are told to study to show ourselves to be approved to God (2 Tim. 2:15). We need to be transformed (Rom. 12:2). Do we study or even read God's Word? Jesus Christ is the Word of God, so reading the Bible as a believer amounts to putting on the mind of Christ. That shows that our minds are not perfect yet.

Therefore, only the spirits of those who accept Jesus Christ are actually **perfect**. Christians can mature by studying the Bible and obeying it.

If we think we can just get by in life without understanding God's ways and requirements, we will be tragically mistaken. Why would God instruct us to study His Word? It is because our lives depend upon it.

We may or may not understand what we hear in church or elsewhere about the requirements for salvation. Our final exam will be the same for everyone. Many will fail. God will be the One who will be deciding by our faith on earth if we pass on into heaven as perfect spirits or not. There is no second chance like the man in the math class had after he had failed the first time.

XI

LOVE ON GOD

Once I got in fairly late at my parents' home where I was staying. My parents were also caring for my brother's three children at the time. My brother's youngest was a very young girl who was laid out in the living room on a quilt pallet. As I passed by, my niece noticed me.

I figured she should have been asleep already. She called to me. I went to see what she needed. She just said, "I want you." To this day, I think she was just worried because she could not calm down enough to get to sleep.

I replied that she could not have me, meaning I was tired and was going to bed myself. Little did I know how awful that probably sounded to a little girl who may have been scared. How I had responded to her bothered me over the years. I think I should have stayed momentarily to see what she had to say and if she was scared.

Many years later, she grew up and overcame some serious hardships. It still grieves me. She arrived once at our house for a graduation party for our oldest daughter, but I was trying to be polite to other guests at the time. Neither I nor my wife got around to talk to her before she left. That grieved me immensely.

A while back I heard that my niece's house had burned with everything in it. I did not even know where she lived, but she lived probably within a twenty mile radius of where we lived. I never heard where the family moved after the fire.

Quite recently, I suddenly discovered that my niece was in a hospital in intensive care. I contacted a relative to try to find more information about which hospital my niece was in so I could check on her.

To my shock, I was informed that my niece had died in the hospital. I still get tears even today when I think of her. It was almost like no one was ever able to reach out to her to comfort her or listen to her. What did that little girl want from me when I was too callous to stop to listen to a child in need?

Because Jesus Christ is the Word of God, the Bible should mean a lot to every Christian. The Word of God consists of both the Old Testament and the New Testament, not just the New Testament.

I have heard or read of many false teachings today, so that correlates with our already living in the end times. I have a list of over seventy false teachings I know of which have occurred during my lifetime. Because there are many lying and seducing spirits at work today, each of us needs to read and study the Word of God.

Perhaps there is a correlation relationship between our reading the Bible and Ezekiel 3:1-3 and Revelation 10:9.

Moreover he said unto me, Son of man, eat that thou findest; eat this roll, and go speak unto the house of Israel. So I opened my mouth, and he caused me to eat that roll. And he said unto me, Son of man, cause thy belly to eat, and fill thy bowels with this roll that I give thee. Then did I eat it; and it was in my mouth as honey for sweetness (Ezek. 3:1-3).

"And I went unto the angel, and said unto him, Give me the little book. And he said unto me, Take it, and eat it up; and it shall make thy belly bitter, but it shall be in thy mouth sweet as honey" (Rev. 10:9).

Regardless, now is a time when Christians need to know the

truth personally in order to guard their hearts from being deceived.

Just to point out one recent error being taught, consider this: One man taught that we do not have to give thanks for all things. What does the Bible state? "Giving thanks always **for all things** unto God and the Father in the name of our Lord Jesus Christ; submitting yourselves one to another in the fear of God" (Eph. 5:20-21). The man's teaching was a blatant contradiction of the Bible. Arm yourselves with the knowledge and wisdom of God.

Today there is a pestilence called the coronavirus, also known as covid-19. Many people have died from it, but the number of deaths has been skewed because doctors have to use their best judgment in listing cause of death. Many of the deaths have probably been caused by multiple issues.

After I read one article of a nurse who volunteered to help in New York, I was fairly shocked to read her accounts of how the sick were not being cared for properly there. As a result of covid-19, government regulations have come forth demanding certain requirements of populations. Some of those requirements have been labeled as being unconstitutional by some people. Those requirements seem to some people to be a ramping up toward a one-world government. They feel that the Constitution of the United States is being subjugated to these regulations, some of which are not even law. It is time to draw near to God, Christian. The dangers in these end times have increased.

Here is that important scripture again to read and remember. "And we know that all things work together for good to them that love God, to them who are the called according to his purpose" (Rom. 8:28).

I do not know how all things work for the good of all of us Christians, but I do believe God's Word. We have a right to believe it or not. If we start choosing parts of the Bible to eliminate just because we do not understand them, then we are in serious trouble.

We have to be prepared to withstand trials, tribulations, and persecutions. I hope all of us are prepared to give thanks for all things now. We can expect the world to get worse even if there is a world-wide revival.

Look at what the Lord said to Jerusalem:

O Jerusalem, Jerusalem, thou that killest the prophets, and stonest them which are sent unto thee, how often would I have gathered thy children together, even as a hen gathereth her chickens under her wings, and ye would not! Behold, your house is left unto you desolate. For I say unto you, Ye shall not see me henceforth, till ye shall say, Blessed is he that cometh in the name of the Lord (Matt. 23:37-39).

Each person is responsible for their own Christian growth once they reach an age of maturity. We cannot just rely upon our pastor's faith or his knowledge of the Bible. We must seriously begin to feed ourselves the Word of God.

God does not want us to have to go to hell. That is why Jesus Christ died for our sins. Do not be careless about salvation. Scripture states that the righteous are scarcely saved. Think of faith as hanging by a thread. If so, would we deal so carelessly about our destination for eternity? God loves us. We need to love on Him and be extremely thankful to Him.

There is more to the story about my niece. I cried more for her than for anyone else of my relatives that have died, even my parents whom I dearly love. I did not know if she knew Jesus Christ, so I told God I was not going to ask if she made it to heaven. I did tell Him that if He had anything He wanted to tell me, I would be glad to hear it. Very quickly after that, I heard God say, "She is with Me."

Life is full of terrible things. I could not make it through life without God. He loves us so much and cares for His faithful ones after their deaths. "Greater love hath no man than this, that a man lay down his life for his friends" (John 15:13).

XII

How Do We Respond?

I know a man who traveled to Israel with a group led by a nationally known minister. They visited one church with a shrine where Jesus was supposedly born. The leader warned the group to be careful not to let any religious spirits get on them.

The man didn't know how one could tell if any spirit was getting on him or anyone else. The group looked around for a short while and then left.

No more was spoken about religious spirits attacking people. The trip was quite full of sights to see. Later in life, the man traveled outside the USA some more. Nothing seemed wrong for the longest time.

Eventually, however, something began to happen that seemed to have no explanation. At irregular intervals, this man began to have brief sessions where he would have to struggle to try to get enough air. He wondered at times if he was going to die for lack of oxygen. A doctor prescribed a strong cough medicine, but it did not stop the sessions of struggling for air.

The man and his wife decided to go to a spiritually qualified friend that they knew who could do deliverance. She invited them into her home. As they sat at her kitchen table, the lady began to calmly command a spirit to come out of the man. He said it was only about five or ten minutes until he was freed from the spirit.

It had been a religious spirit. The man had no idea about

how it had attached itself to him, but he did remember what the minister had said to the group in Israel. They had been warned not to let any religious spirit get on them.

God does not want anyone to perish. However, many already have. It is important to understand what is required to be saved. In fact, it is too important to disregard.

God said that many are called, but few are chosen. God wants everyone saved, but His righteous requirements must be met. He also stated that those who will be with Him throughout eternity will be those who are called, chosen, and faithful. We must remain faithful to Him.

Warnings are very plain in the Bible that we all need to understand. Faith in Jesus Christ is the only way to Father God. Judas Iscariot was one of the original apostles, yet he betrayed Jesus Christ and never repented. Another man, Demas, was noted in the book Philemon (written about the year 62 AD) by the apostle Paul as being a fellow laborer with Paul. However, in 2 Timothy (written about the year 67 AD), Paul stated that Demas had forsaken him and had become one who loved the present world. Anyone who loves the world is an enemy of God.

The parable of the sower in Matthew 13 and Mark 4 is very important. It plainly indicates that it is possible to hear the Word of God but not understand it and thus never be saved.

Some people may hear the Word and immediately receive it and believe, yet fall away when affliction, tribulation, or persecution arises. Still others may hear the Word, but cares of the world, the deceitfulness of riches, and the lusts of other things choke the Word so that it becomes unfruitful.

Those in the fourth group hear the Word and become spiritually fruitful. Note that the second group actually believed for a while before they fell away.

Other scriptures indicate the possibility of many people

thinking they are saved when in actuality they are not. The parable of the ten virgins in Matthew 25 indicates half had enough oil, a symbol of the Holy Spirit, to be able to enter heaven, whereas the other five who did not have enough oil were never granted the opportunity to enter heaven.

Matthew 7 has an extremely important message. Verse 21 plainly states that only those who do the will of God will be able to enter heaven, yet in verses 22-23 we are told that many who claim to have done works for God, such as prophesying in His name and casting out devils, will be told that God never knew them. They will be told to depart from God since they are workers of iniquity.

Observe the following scripture carefully:

*Even thus shall it be in the day when the Son of man is revealed. In that day, he which shall be upon the housetop, and his stuff in the house, let him not come down to take it away: and he that is in the field, let him likewise not return back. Remember Lot's wife. Whosoever shall seek to save his life shall lose it; and whosoever shall lose his life shall preserve it. I tell you, in that night there shall be two men in one bed; the one shall be taken, and the other shall be left. Two **women** shall be grinding together; the one shall be taken, and the other left. Two **men** shall be in the field; the one shall be taken, and the other left* (Luke 17:30-36).

Notice these verses speak of the day when Jesus Christ is revealed. The bolded words, "men" and "women," are not actually a part of scripture. The living Christians will not be caught up until the dead in Christ are caught up to Jesus, and we are plainly told of two true prophets in the book of Revelation who will die in the seven year tribulation period. That means that the catching up of living Christians will not occur until at least after those two prophets are raised up from death.

Scripture warns us to not be deceived or to even deceive ourselves. You can use scripture to understand scripture, but it is not right to just take a scripture such as 1 Thessalonians 4:16-17 and claim that it will happen at a certain time without proof. We have been warned that there would be false teachers and doctrines in the end times, and the end times began at least as early as the day of Pentecost the year that Jesus died.

Do we still think we are truly prepared for the day of our mortal death or the day when Jesus returns? Have we been watching and praying as the Lord instructed? Are we truly a doer of God's Word? Has our spiritual life in Christ grown cold?

Cold is far below lukewarm, and the lukewarm in the Laodicean church in Revelation 3 were warned that if they did not repent, then they would be spewed out of Jesus' mouth. That would place those people outside of Jesus. Christians are those who are both in Christ and have Christ in themselves. We have to take stock of our relationship with Jesus Christ. Are we worrying about our daily needs and desires? Are we so affected by what people of this world think of us that we have already denied Christ? Is our affection on things of this world, or is it set on things above?

Have we just sat in church or Sunday school and listened, or have we really put forth effort to read and study the Word of God for ourselves? Do we reverence God enough so that we strive to ensure we are right with God in our hearts and daily thoughts and actions?

If we love this world and money, then we need to repent now. If we love either of them, then we hate God. God does not want us to have to burn forever in the lake of fire, the second death. He wants us to have an abundant life, which is a life with righteousness, peace, and joy in the Holy Spirit inside us.

Have we remained faithful to God? We need to check our own hearts to see if we have lasting faith in Jesus Christ. Eternity in the lake of fire is to be avoided by taking action immediately before we die!

Church was not meant to be just Christians sitting while pastors do all the spiritual work. We are too far into the end times to be about our ease. Spirits of apathy and complacency seem to have overwhelmed much of the church spiritually.

Ephesians 6:12 states that we wrestle with evil spiritual principalities, powers, rulers, and wickedness. Why do we think God told us to put on His full armor? (Eph. 6:13-18) There is a spiritual war that has been going on for thousands of years.

Why do we think God provided the Holy Spirit to comfort and help us? At times when we do not know how to pray, we can let the Holy Spirit pray through us. That gifting of speaking in tongues comes with the baptism of the Holy Spirit. It is holy.

If we have not received such giftings from God, we can ask Him for them. Just as in physical war, there are casualties; so in spiritual war, there are also casualties. We have to defend ourselves and our families.

God's house is to be a house of prayer. Each Christian's body is the temple of God (1 Cor. 3:16). We can apply ourselves to fill our temple, our body, with prayer. Get to know God, for He said His sheep hear His voice and know Him (John 10:14, 27).

Christians are to progress from spiritual babies into youth and then into adults. Eternal rewards are to be given on judgment day. While we are still mortal, we should put forth effort to grow spiritually. Read your Bible. Learn to ask God questions and listen to His answers.

We can learn to do spiritual warfare and enter into deep spiritual worship of our eternal Creator. Life and death are in the power of our tongues (Prov. 18:21). Let's learn to bless people with our words. Don't neglect to pray for souls to get saved, for our words and prayers may be used to win souls to Christ Jesus.

We have to be spiritually alert and ready daily to face dangers. If an evil spirit can come upon some of us and choke us, we are vulnerable people, yet the Holy Spirit in us is greater than the evil spirits. The warnings in scripture are for all of us.

Spiritual maturity should be the goal for all of us. It takes work, but God is more than willing to help us progress.

Bibliography

The Companion Bible. Grand Rapids: Kregel, 1990.

Parsons, John J. "The Significance of the Shofar." 2009. 31 Oct. 2016 <www.hebrew4christians.com/Holidays/Fall_Holidays/Elul/Shofar/shofar.html>.

Meyers, Rick. e-Sword. [Franklin, TN] Vers. 10.4.0. July 2014. 1 Jan. 2017<www.e-sword.net>.

Strong, James. *The Exhaustive Concordance of the Bible.* Nashville: Abingdon, 1978 ed.

Webster's Seventh New Collegiate Dictionary. Springfield, Mass.: G. & C. Merriam, 1963 ed.

Willmington, Harold L. *Willmington's Complete Guide to Bible Knowledge: Old Testament Survey.* Wheaton, IL: Tyndale House, 1992.

About the Author

WAYNE BELCHER, called by God while still in high school, began to seek God after graduation from college. He had a great hunger for God and His Word but saw no power in the church. Throughout about 40 years of secular work, Wayne studied and prepared himself for these end times. He has a great passion to see the church walking in truth, righteousness, and power. Wayne and his wife, Kathleen, are parents of two daughters and one adopted son.

To contact the author: belcher.wayne@gmail.com

CPSIA information can be obtained
at www.ICGtesting.com
Printed in the USA
BVHW040831080721
611351BV00012B/1449